Balanced Website Design

WITHDRAWN

Dave Lawrence and Soheyla Tavakol

Balanced Website Design

Optimising Aesthetics, Usability and Purpose

 Springer

Dave Lawrence, BSc, MA, PhD, PGCertHE
Middlesex University
London
UK

Soheyla Tavakol, BA, MA, PGCertHE,
Middlesex University
London
UK

British Library Cataloguing in Publication Data
A catalogue record for this book is available from the British Library

Library of Congress Control Number: 2006928131

ISBN-10: 1-84628-518-6
ISBN-13: 978-1-84628-518-9

Printed on acid-free paper

9 8 7 6 5 4 3 2 1

Springer Science+Business Media
springer.com

I dedicate this book to my old dog, Sheber, and my Dad – both taking a walk in the sky

Dave Lawrence, BSc, PhD, MA, PGCertHE
School of Computing, Middlesex University, London, UK

To my beautiful Bali

Soheyla Tavakol, BA, MA, PGCertHE
School of Computing, Middlesex University, London, UK

PREFACE

The intention here is to introduce the book by summarising the following aspects:

- Purpose of the book
- Main features of the process described (BWD)
- Audience targeted
- Way the book is to be used
- Features of the book website
- Author background information

Introduction

This book has been conceived to help you with the process of designing a website by providing the structured framework of a website design methodology. It does not give tutorials in technical work, such as HTML or DHTML, in editing images or other media, in setting up database processing, or in scripting. Other books do this very well already.

The scope of this book is to explain the context of the website design activity and to provide easy-to-follow steps in the process of website design itself supported by a comprehensive set of design documentation tools. It gives you the structure to apply your technical, analytical, and creative skills in a very effective and focussed manner. The approach described in the book is relevant for individual and team designer/developers and for any type of website envisaged.

The process described in this book has been given the name 'Balanced Website Design' (BWD), the notion partly being that a holistic balanced approach is needed for any design and implementation project to be successful. More specifically, the process described has a substantial emphasis on balancing the identification of detailed design needs with the derivation of closely associated design ideas to satisfy those needs. There is also equal weight given to optimising aesthetic, usability, and purpose characteristics of the target website. Each of these aspects is considered important and vital for success.

The process described aims to help you achieve real tangible benefits in terms of websites that are appropriate and successful – matching detailed identified needs and desires through careful and thorough design. New perspectives on website usability and aesthetics are also explored and discussed in dedicated chapters.

The book describes the background and context of BWD, as well as working through the implementation of the methodology in detail, step by step.

Main Features

Balanced Website Design comprises a set of steps that collectively form a coherent, structured pathway beginning at the inception of project ideas/request through website implementation. It uses well-proven characteristics of the classic 'Waterfall' and prototyping approaches, infuses important new elements, and applies perspectives that relate specifically to website design.

Crucially, BWD has a focus on identifying and satisfying specific needs that relate to what are regarded as the core aspects of website design – purpose, usability, and aesthetics. The dynamic use of documentation plays a substantial role in BWD – to assist with the activity of designing as well as to record the ideas, findings, and decisions made (for later reflection and iterative design). There is a complete set of specially designed documentation templates for active use across all of the design steps – facilitating thoroughness and cohesiveness and promoting consistency across different projects and between project team members.

In the chapters on usability and aesthetics, the material includes an introduction to the notions of 'straight' and 'curved' usability, a set of enhanced usability heuristics, and a fresh analysis of what is meant by the term 'aesthetic'. The discussion helps us explore the notion of beauty in the complex world of website design and how attention to aesthetics intertwines with that needed to be given to usability and purpose functionality.

The process described has built-in flexibility and has user centred characteristics such as that experienced in 'soft systems' approaches, plus the robustness and rigour found in established structured information systems methodologies. New ideas and innovative approaches are moulded into BWD, informed by long experience in web technology, web design, digital media, graphic design, and general information systems.

Audience Targeted

Balanced Website Design is both for the experienced website developer and the novice or intermediate developers. Everyone likes an approach that is

- easy to follow,
- gives coherence and structure,
- makes for relevant, appropriate, and effective designs,
- reduces risks of incompleteness and unsuitability, and
- makes the whole process more straightforward and robust.

The format, structure, and scope of the book are designed to be particularly suitable for use by tutors and students as part of any undergraduate or pre-graduate course studying or relating to website design. The process is also appropriate for nonacademic use.

BWD is suitable for individual and team projects and is applicable to all types and genres of websites. It does, however, require that there be technical/creative skills available commensurate with the tasks of creating/generating design ideas, building code (and/or using code-generating software), and preparing the content of the website. The requirements of the website must be known, or there must be analysis skills available and access to sources of that information. BWD comprehensively facilitates and helps secure a strong and relevant website design/implementation, but the responsibility and power of design creativity are firmly retained by the analyst/designer/client.

Way the Book Is to Be Used

The book is divided into sections, grouping together chapters dealing with related activities and topics. Section 1 (Chapters 1–4) is likely to be used as reference material on the first reading of the book and then subsequently as periodic refresher material. The section introduces the main features of BWD and places the process into a wider context. The chapters on usability and aesthetics provide new insights into these topic areas to help in the creation of effective designs.

Section 2 describes the details of the methodology steps, so these chapters (5–8) are likely to be used directly over and over again. Section 3 is essentially a reference section, with technical guidance on software tools (Chapter 9) and a look at options and issues relating to hosting and website management (Chapter 10).

At strategic points, the book includes tutorial, seminar, and case study questions. The tutorial and seminar questions are optional but are especially recommended if you are following an academic course and will help reinforce understanding. Case study exercises are also provided to enable you to practice the details of the methodology by applying each step in turn to your own chosen website development project. Example uses of the documentation are given within the relevant chapters to help with understanding and clarity.

The Book's Website

A website will be available (to coincide with the book's publication) to provide resource support for readers and users of the BWD methodology. The website (www.springer.com/1-84628-518-6) will include the following:

- downloadable copies of design documentation templates,
- further case study examples of BWD use,
- a designers' message forum,
- BWD hints and tips,
- errata and addenda (regarding the book text).

Author Backgrounds

Dr. Dave Lawrence is a senior lecturer in multimedia web technology and digital media (Middlesex University, London, UK), leader of a level 2 web design module for over five years, and has widely published and presented research in this field and in the related area of interactive design. Following several years as an information systems analyst/designer in consultancy organisations, he became an academia-based lecturer, researcher, and practitioner. His experience in website design goes back to the mid-1990's when implementing early 'live' Internet video/audio broadcasts. His current collaborative projects include the design of a conceptual multi-media virtual website and exploring web streaming/digital technology in interactive arts contexts.

Soheyla Tavakol (senior lecturer, Middlesex University, London, UK) is a specialist in aesthetics and lectures in website design and digital media. Experience in the arts and in graphic design, plus a computer science perspective, contribute to the author's unique awareness of aesthetics and design in digital and Web contexts.

ACKNOWLEDGMENTS

We thank our families for their assistance and support over the years and for their patience in allowing us to spend the time living this book.

Thank you to Bob Fields for feedback on the usability chapter and to Satinder Gill and Colin Tully for inspirations and lifelines.

A special thank you to Filiz Karabey, who kindly allowed us to base our case study examples on the design of her first-ever website – a coursework project that was part of a level 2 undergraduate website design module. We also very much appreciate the various website owners who allowed us to present screenshots of their webpages in our chapters discussing usability and aesthetics. Thanks go to Rosebud Productions for help with book cover imagery.

A big thank you to Helen Callaghan and Catherine Brett of Springer-Verlag for the invitation to write this book and for their unending support and help in traveling through the complex process of preparing it for publication. A special thanks to Michael Koy (Senior Production Editor) and the whole production team at Springer New York for their valuable contributions to bringing this book to physical fruition.

London, UK   Dave Lawrence
London, UK   Soheyla Tavakol

CONTENTS

Section 1: Grounding

CHAPTER ONE

Balanced Website Design (BWD): The Context Explained

Overview

This chapter establishes the need to consider the use of a website design methodology and describes features desired in an effective methodology. A process of web design and implementation that follows principles identified as being necessary in a website design methodology is introduced and summarised. The process (BWD – Balanced Website Design) has a focus on balancing detailed design needs with specific design ideas. It adopts a comprehensive, structured, and stepped approach and optimises the combination of appropriate aesthetic, usability, and purpose characteristics by detailed analysis and design.

Give and Gain

This chapter will take about 40 minutes to read, plus time for the exercises at the end, and will help you gain the following important aspects:

- an appreciation of why structured design methodologies are generally useful,
- an awareness of features desired in a website design methodology,
- an understanding of the core features and overall structure of BWD.

You need to read this chapter to bridge the gap between general awareness of approaches to website design and the details of the methodology process described later in this book (Section 2). The chapter establishes a context for considering the details of a website design methodology and explains the fundamental features and concept of BWD.

Website Design – Historical Perspective

The first webpages, albeit mainly plain text pages, began to be created in the early 1990s. All design and implementation at that time was, understandably, on an ad hoc basis, with little in the way of standards yet established; there was no pattern of acceptable styles and approaches. At the same time, however, expectations (in terms of content and technical complexity), audience volumes, and technical possibilities were relatively limited.

Approaches and techniques were initially simplistic, with webpages comprising mainly text and with little attention to visual layout design, detailed usability, and quality dynamic content provision. These 'design' attributes were not really an issue of particular concern at the time, though, as it was still at the experimental technical 'leading edge' to create and use a webpage.

Now, in this fast-developing field, it is approximately a decade later, and all website designers are faced with massive commercial and personal expectations, extensive technical and design options, and a continuing surge of interest and investment in the World Wide Web (the 'Web') across all societies and communities.

Rapidly, we have all traveled through a period of dramatic expansion and explosion in web activity – the Internet is now so prominent in our lives – for work, fun, and just about anything to do with living.

The Web is proving to be a fantastic breakthrough in this world of technology and the Internet. It means that now we all have powerful access to using and developing webpages – providing a great array of opportunities to individuals and organisations. Every website owner/developer, on a global basis, is enabled to

- express a feeling or an idea,
- promote a business,
- market a product,
- form a community,
- help others,
- have fun,
- encourage exploration,
- promote or trigger a new interest,
- distribute and/or access information,
- experiment with new technology,
- be independent,
- be global.

Running a good website in this first decade of the 21st century is rather like running a car in the 1950s and 1960s–it provides a surge of personal power and possibilities, reaching places that are excitingly new and previously might have been exclusive or difficult to access. The huge, and somewhat unique, bonus is that we also inherently benefit from the collective presence of the myriad of other websites (a bit like individual mobile phones being much more influential and useful now that general use and market penetration is so widespread and that the technology for mobile multimedia is becoming a reality). Websites in the same genre do compete for attention, however, as do mobile phones and their users.

For almost any idea, activity, or interest, there is a website – each needing to be designed and created. If you have already faced these tasks, you will know that however powerful the software that is used to build the pages, the issue of getting the design 'right' can still be a nightmare – getting it to look and work appropriately. Managing the process and keeping 'in control' is not easy, especially with the massive range of technology and content possibilities, the demands and pressures of the marketplace, and the idiosyncrasies of the technology and of us as people using the Web.

For many of the past years, partly due to the relative newness of the activity of creating websites and partly due to the ease of access to website creation software, the tendency has been for websites to be designed and implemented without the adoption of a clear method, and rarely with a recognised structured methodology. Increasingly, particularly over the last two or three years, interest has been emerging (in publications and website design practice) in adopting approaches that have more effectiveness and give the designer more control. The use of a comprehensive and specifically designed approach to website design is becoming recognised as important.

Without a structured approach, it is likely that the delivered aims and scope of the site will be incomplete. Intuitive skills and deep experience can sometimes offset any damage brought about by not adopting a structured approach, but the risks are high. If there is a lack of detailed analysis and design, it is unlikely that the style, scope, and content will be satisfactory. The use of existing websites as guides or templates is a temptation, and this can perpetuate the use of inappropriate designs – particularly as the most 'basic' designs are often the easiest to reuse by the nonspecialist designer.

Poorly designed websites, lacking focus and purposeful design, are at best of minimal use and time wasting and at worst damaging and financially corrosive. We encourage you to use a structured and methodological approach to your website design work to help you optimise your designs and maximise the strength of the actual implementations.

The only reason not to study and take up a structured design approach is if you are already

- *entirely* happy with the design of your websites,
- *entirely* confident that you have a tried, trusted, and consistent approach to satisfy all (website) needs, and
- *entirely* satisfied that your site users/clients are impressed by your websites and the design approach.

The price to be paid for producing a poor website is getting higher and higher – in terms of missed opportunities, lost revenues, damaged reputations, etc. The Web is a busy place (with lots of competition), and web users have ever-rising expectations and can very quickly move to an alternative website if satisfaction and/or interest is not speedily and substantially achieved. Potential audiences don't want to waste time with sites that appear amateurish or are confusing, uninteresting, or inappropriate – there are so many others from which to choose, and all only a few clicks away.

Table 1.1: Desired features of a design methodology

- A conceptual base, which is clearly reflected in the framework of tasks and the process itself
- Demonstrably having a depth and scope that are comprehensive and vital for successful design and implementation
- Design documentation that triggers creative and effective design ideas, makes evaluation of designs and outcome effectiveness sufficiently objective, helps developer team understanding and awareness, and eases the task of site maintenance, growth, and enhancement
- Provides/enables template designs and encap-sulates good practice for use in subsequent projects
- Encourages professional and academic impro-vement in the design/implementation process

The term 'methodology' is derived from the Greek words *meta* (following) and *hodos* (the way) [1] A software design methodology is by definition an organised, documented set of procedures and guidelines for one or more phases of a software life cycle [2] A design methodology should be more than a set of useful tasks, more than a collection of 'good advice' – it must have a conceptual base and a comprehensive set of steps that are integrated and supported by a documentation process. It is our view that a good design methodology must include certain general features (Table 1.1).

Website Design – An Emerging Theme

In recent years, several published guidelines and approaches have been recommended for website designers (e.g., [3], [4], [5], [6]). An analysis of these publications, and general observational and practitioner experience, reveal an emerging theme (Table 1.2) for good website design.

Table 1.2: An emerging theme for good website design

- A website should have a clear overall purpose.
- The design and content should reflect the needs of the target audience and purpose of the site.
- The design should aim at creating an appropriate visual layout and 'mood' for the site (the aesthetics).
- Usability is very important – typically targeting simplicity and clarity.
- Adopting a user (audience) centred design process is effective good practice.
- Documentation (diagrammatic and descriptive format) needs to carried out as part of the process.
- Appropriate navigation styles and relevant content are crucial characteristics of a website.
- Prototyping and iteration are encouraged in the process.
- A structured, stepped approach is favoured.
- Testing of designs and implementations must be carried out.

In this competitive digital world, it is essential to strive for high website quality – to create websites that satisfy the required purpose(s), have a magnetic aesthetic, and have a level of usability that makes it a suitable experience (in 'operational' terms). A good website design methodology must be designed in such a way that it will help the designer achieve this quality by providing a process to identify detailed needs, apply appropriately detailed design ideas, and evaluate the outcomes – all within a structured framework.

This book introduces a framework that is designed to allow accepted good practice in the details of website design/implementation tasks to be brought together into a structured process. The methodology is based on the concept of identifying key design needs (across a combination of target aesthetic, usability, and purpose characteristics) and balancing these needs with specific design ideas. A stepped and comprehensive approach is adopted to optimize the aesthetic, usability, and purpose characteristics of the target website. An aim of the described process is to make it generally understandable, approachable, and usable.

Now, don't run away with the idea that this is easy. It is never going to be easy to produce something that has to combine creative and technical flair in an environment as competitive as the Internet. A structured website design methodology can help, but as with any development methodology, and with any project type, success requires skills inherent to the process, innovativeness, discipline, and motivation to take advantage of the structured guidance.

The cost/benefit ratio of utilising a methodology such as BWD is very attractive – the extra cost for a project is relatively low (the main investment items being an instructional book, possibly a few days of training in process techniques, and thoughtful care taken in the various stages of a website project). Compare this small outlay with the repeated and substantial benefits of producing very relevant and effective websites – benefits enjoyed perhaps on a purely financial basis (e.g., retail or subscription terms) and/or on the basis of the website providing greater influence, a richer experience, more enjoyment, and/or increased interest. Any methodology, by definition, needs some dedicated time to be taken in its use (because any methodology has rules, a conceptual basis, and sequences of steps that all need to be understood and followed carefully before substantial benefits are realised). The time needed should be regarded as an investment ahead of gaining the long-term benefits of quality and efficiency.

Balanced Website Design (BWD) – An Overview

Increasingly, the importance of aesthetics and usability in website design is being recognised by experts, users, and developers [9]. Together with the intrinsic purpose needs of the website, these aspects form the three pillars of website design and hence the BWD methodology (Fig. 1.1).

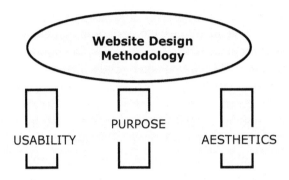

Fig. 1.1: Website design: the three pillars

The precise nature, extent, and specific characteristics desired of each aspect will depend on the genre and particular aspirations for the website in question, and the derivation of this information is achieved by thorough requirements analysis.

BWD has been designed to reinforce and develop the 'emerging theme' suggested in Table 1.2 and satisfy the general design methodology requirements set out in Table 1.1. The methodology encompasses and progresses the art of good and effective website design by incorporating additional features with attributes found in traditional development approaches (see Table 1.3).

Table 1.3: Characteristic features of BWD

- A top-down structured and user-centred approach
- Emphasis on website aesthetics, usability, and purpose as the critical components of any website and website design
- A set of design steps that lead and support a developer from commencement to project completion – adapted from the well-proven 'Waterfall' framework and utilising checkpoints and iterative prototyping
- Adopting a detailed approach of identifying specific needs and corresponding specific design ideas
- Unique documentation notation, styled to encourage a structured, comprehensive, reusable, and transparent approach to the design work
- An expansion on traditional usability considerations (to cater more clearly to *all* types of websites)
- Uncovering perspectives on the topic of aesthetics and its relation to good website design
- A comprehensive stepped process and approach that is easy to follow and easy to understand

In summary, the BWD methodology can be seen as a combination of traditional and innovative aspects that are underpinned by a structured stepped process assisted by specially constructed design documentation techniques (see Fig. 1.2).

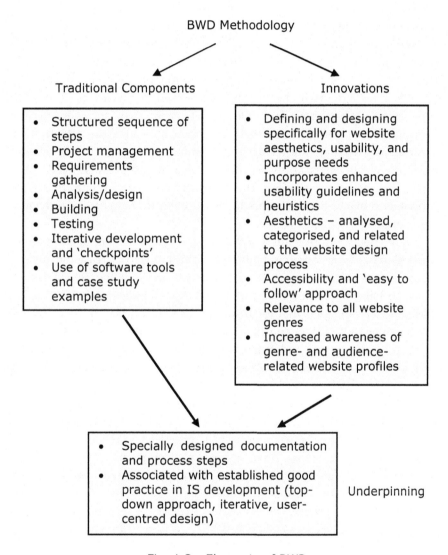

Fig. 1.2: Elements of BWD

If you have experience in the wider field of software development and methodologies that support general information systems, you will recognise that certain aspects of BWD relate to aspects of traditional approaches to design/development. This is so that the process can include the strengths of such approaches and also because a website is in fact an information system (IS).

BWD incorporates an adapted 'waterfall' [11] approach (where a development project is broken down into a series of related sequential steps leading to a conclusion) and the notion of iterative prototyping (where ideas are tried, tested, and improved in cycles as a project progresses). When you look closely at each step and the design documentation, you will see that there is a built-in acute attention to ascertaining detailed knowledge and understanding about the characteristic website needs, applying creative ideas to satisfy those needs, and managing the whole process. There are periodic checkpoints to reflect formally on plans and prototypes to check that requirements are fully and appropriately satisfied.

All the detail and reasoning of the design is documented, in addition to the design needs, as the project advances. This helps to increase the quality of the actual work (helping the designer to carry out the actual design tasks) and also makes it a transparent process. As indicated in Fig. 1.3, an additional advantage is that the documented design ideas and analysis of needs can be reused in, or contribute to, future website design projects.

Website developers and teams who follow and utilise BWD will not only produce very effective and appropriate websites but there will also be an important air of consistency – not only within the website itself but also across and between different website projects. This is extremely useful in building up a good reputation for quality and helps when teams and developers move between projects. Consistency in this context means that the approach across projects, and project teams, is recognisably similar and that design differences between implemented websites relate to the differing particular design needs.

Depending on your background and experience, potentially you can benefit from using a process such as BWD in different ways:

- **Experienced and successful website designers** – BWD has the potential of making your websites *more* successful, *more* appropriate, and *more* effective. It will increase and sharpen the focus you already give to understanding detailed and important website requirements and turning that awareness into real and

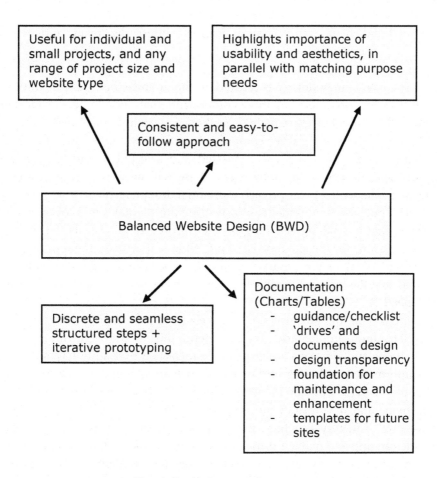

Fig. 1.3: Main BWD features

specific design characteristics. The design documentation potentially will speed up future projects due to the potential re-use of good design ideas.

- **Inexperienced/novice website designers** – BWD provides the comfort and stability of a structured and inspiring environment that boosts confidence and enables effective results to be achieved from the very first project.

- **Development** *teams* – a consistent environment is provided for design and implementation, which helps with the practical work and helps with communication within the team and with users/clients.

The BWD methodology is centred on the premise that to create a fully effective website, there are three components that need to be considered carefully and comprehensively – aesthetics, usability, and purpose. The requirements for these three components must be identified in detail and then particular design ideas generated and selected to satisfy each of those specific needs. In many cases, there will be two or more design ideas implemented to target each individual design need.

The purpose requirements of a website are pivotal – it is around this aspect that everything else hinges. The purpose requirements tell us the main reasons for the site to exist at all. What is it actually there to do? To achieve? What should the user of the site be able to do or make happen? What are the key deliverables of the website (to the user and to the owner)?

Identifying the purpose(s) of the website at first might seem to be an obvious and simple task. To an extent, this is true – certainly, the intentions and aims of a website can be identified by traditional methods of information gathering and analysis. In many situations this will be a simple exercise but not in others, such as where there are conflicting opinions and priorities of multiple stakeholders in a website. A further potential difficulty is where the purposes of the website become very wide-ranging and make it difficult to arrive at a succinct and coherent set of requirements. It is essential that purpose requirements of the website be clearly identified and then fully satisfied by the website design.

The desired aesthetics and usability characteristics must also be targeted by the website design, but by the very nature of these two complex aspects it is much more difficult to fully and unquestionably ascertain requirements and satisfy targeted needs. Our views on usability and aesthetics are discussed in detail in Chapters 3 and 4, including much more about categorisation, evaluation, and their interdependence. Usability, of software in general and more recently of websites, is a topic that still enjoys extensive interest and research. Numerous publications detail what is deemed to be good usability [4, 7, 8, 9, 10, 12], and this work is taken on board by BWD as a starting point and foundation for the treatment of usability. We suggest categorisations of website genre and scenarios, introduce the concepts of 'straight' and 'curved' usability (more on this in Chapter 3), and derive a simple set of heuristics (rationalised and extended from existing work in this area). We have embarked on a broad research study of aesthetics through the perspective of website design, and initial findings are discussed in Chapter 4.

The specific aesthetic needs are likely to differ greatly from one site to another (particularly in different genres), with usability needs comprising a mix of core 'good usability' standard requirements common to most sites plus specific usability needs for that particular website and website genre. To an extent, websites group themselves into genres and sub-sections of genres – but even within such groupings, each website will (or should) have unique sets of needs and design ideas utilised in the targeting of those needs. The balance of the amount, nature, and intensity of aesthetic and usability needs will vary from website to website – some sites will demand a greater emphasis on usability issues, others on aesthetics. In all cases, these two aspects are intertwined, and they have to be considered in conjunction – as decisions about one will almost always have an impact on the other.

Purpose, usability, and aesthetic needs of a website have to be identified early in the project cycle of designing and implementing a website. Progressively, the design process has to refine and crystallise those three sets of needs and evolve a website design that targets and achieves the combined set of requirements. In BWD, a specially designed supportive set of documentation tools help you travel through the process of designing and implementing your website – documentation that helps you design more effectively and is also useful for future maintenance and evolution of the site.

BWD itself does not make any decisions or provide specific solutions to particular design aspirations of a website. It does, however, provide the framework and approach for the designer to do that in a comprehensive manner and in a way that maximises potential. There are too many combinations of needs and requirements for any book to list all the ideal answers, and there is never only one way of satisfying design needs. Successful website design owes a substantial degree of its effectiveness to the unique ideas and energy of the designers themselves – and would not benefit in the long term from a centralised 'rule book' of design decisions. Otherwise all websites of particular types would eventually look and feel exactly the same and hence lose the benefits of uniqueness and originality.

BWD – The Structure

There are twelve steps in the BWD methodology cycle, forming four main phases of a website design and implementation project (Table 1.4). These steps are organised into the four phases of Requirements - initial acquisition, design needs – building the picture, designing the solution, and creating the website.

BWD uses a clock metaphor (Fig. 1.4) to help visualise the whole process and keep track of where we are at any point during a project. The twelve steps in BWD are represented by the twelve numbers around the clock face. As the clock hand reaches each new number, this represents our reaching each new stage in the sequence of BWD steps.

Table 1.4: BWD steps

Requirements – initial acquisition
Step 1: Project startup
Step 2: Time and task analysis
Step 3: Initial requirements gathering

Design needs – building the picture
Step 4: Purpose aspirations recognition
Step 5: Usability and aesthetic requirements recognition
Step 6: Review and Reflect (1) – including possible flashbacks

Designing the solution
Step 7: Technical options/selections
Step 8: Navigation design, screen layouts, webpage dialogues, purpose mapping, and content index
Step 9: Review and Reflect (2) – including possible flashbacks

Creating the website
Step 10: Coding and building,
Step 11: Website testing and evaluation
Step 12: User evaluation/Review and Reflect (3) – including possible flashbacks

The clock therefore is a visual indicator of project position and a reminder of the context of each step. A clock is used as the metaphor because there are twelve steps and because the aspects of time, timing, and iterations are important to BWD. Although the clock is divided into equal segments, it is clear that we actually need to spend more time on certain aspects than others – and this will vary from project to project and for different project team configurations. Notice the intermittent 'Review and Reflect' tasks – these are strategically placed so that at key times we appraise how well the project work is targeting effectiveness and real needs.

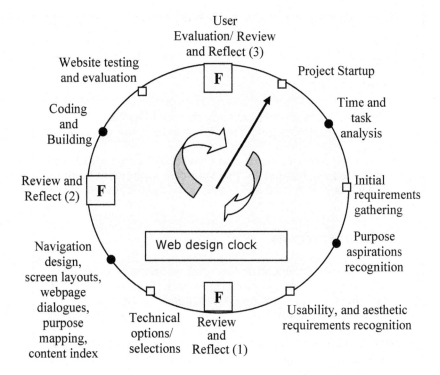

Fig. 1.4: BWD clock metaphor

At each of these three 'Review and Reflect' (R&R) steps, we can take a 'flashback' to earlier steps. The flashback is so that we can go through one or more previous steps again to resolve a problem or deficiency as revealed in the R&R step, producing a new iteration of the design. We then return to the R&R step, and if things are satisfactory we can continue with subsequent steps.

The website design and implementation is completed when the final Review & Reflect task (positioned at the 12 o'clock point on the BWD clock) does not demand any more 'flashbacks' and hence the website is ready to 'go live'.

The twelve steps of BWD are as applicable to small projects as they are to large and complex projects, and are designed to be easy to follow. The steps are discrete and distinct but link together to form a logical project flow.

Chapter Exercises

Seminar Topics

1. Is a website design *methodology* needed? Discuss.
2. To what extent does documentation and/or the documenttation process help or hinder a project?
3. List some typical features and characteristics (e.g., 12–16) of websites you have seen. Use your own judgement to identify each one as a purpose, usability, or aesthetics aspect.

Tutorial Exercises

1. List three or four 'opportunities' that websites can provide – either for users or developers/owners. Surf the Web for example websites providing those 'opportunities'.
2. List three of the key aspects that help form an 'emerging theme' for good website design advice.
3. Write out the list of BWD steps and make estimates of the percentage of project time that you think typically might be spent on each step.

Case Study

1. For your case study website, what 'skills help' do you envisage needing to make sure your website will be totally effective and appropriate?
2. Start thinking about 'project management' – e.g., how will the need for flashbacks (at R&R stages) be decided, and what criteria will be used to decide that the project has reached completion.
3. Of purpose, usability, and aesthetics, try to predict which is likely to be the most significant influence on your project website design.

Chapter References

1. http://www.messagesfromspiritworld.info/UTW/Unification %20Thoughta12.html (accessed April 17, 2004).
2. http://www.hyperdictionary.com/search.aspx?define= methodology (accessed April 17, 2004).
3. Concepcion A. (2002), *Professional Website Design From Start To Finish*, F&W Publications, Cincinnati.
4. Cato J. (2001), *User-Centred Web Design*, Addison-Wesley, Reading, MA.
5. Nierderst J. (2003), *Learning Web Design*, 2nd Edition, O'Reilly, Sebastopol.
6. Knuckles C.D. & Yuen D.S. (2004), Web Applications: Concepts and *Real World Design*, Wiley, New York.
7. Krug S. (2000), *Don't Make Me Think*, New Riders, Indianapolis ISBN: 0-7897-2310-7.
8. Isen J. (1994). "Heuristic Evaluation". In J. Nielsen and R.L. Mack (Eds.), *Usability Inspection Methods*, John Wiley & Sons, New York.
9. Badre A.N. (2002), *Shaping Web Usability*, Addison-Wesley, Reading, MA.
10. Internet & Computing Resource Centre (accessed January 2003), "web usability" mentions Nielsen, Spool, and Krug et al., including a useful list of publications, http://www.asu.edu/jukebox/resources/usability.html
11. Stanford University webpage (accessed January 2003), "Classical Waterfall Methodology", http://www-db. stanford.edu/~burback/water_sluice/sluice6.25.97/ws/node 50.html.
12. Nielsen J. (1999), "*Designing Web Usability: The Practice of Simplicity*", New Riders Publishing, ISBN: 156205810X, Indianapolis, USA.

CHAPTER TWO

The World of Website Design

Overview

This chapter analyses the 'world' of website design, including categorising development scenarios, website genres, and user types to form a background for understanding the process and infrastructure of website design. The general pragmatics of website design and the preparation that might be useful ahead of commencing a website design project are also discussed.

Give and Gain

It will take approximately 45 minutes to read through this chapter, plus time for the exercises at the end. It is expected that you will benefit by

- gaining or reinforcing awareness of the range of typical development scenarios, website categories, and target users,

- further understanding the general approach and pragmatics of website design, and
- being aware of what preparation is necessary in advance of a website design project.

Website Design – Project Context

There are many situations from within which websites are required to be designed and developed. The characteristics of the development scenario and the overall profile of the target website form an initial view of the project environment. These aspects are represented in Fig. 2.1 ('website design – technical context').

The 'technical context' of website design can be divided into the 'development scenario' and the 'website profile'. The development scenario describes whether the development is on an individual basis or a team effort. The skill levels of those developers and whether they are acting as consultants to an external client or it is a personal or in-house project also help to characterise the development scenario. The final factors are the level of technical specification (hardware and software) and the type of website client/owner (commercial or nonprofit organisation – large or small/medium, or individual).

We see the website profile as comprising the genre of the website, the delivery mode (of the items provided by the website), and whether there is a direct cost to the user for any receipt or request of the deliverable item(s) from the website.

The list of website genres that we use, in Fig. 2.1, follows a development and enhancement of the categorisation made by Badre [1]. Additions to that list are the 'activation' and 'experience' type websites. In our categorisations (see Fig. 2.1), there is also a 'hybrid' category of website in that a website could be a mixture of two or more of the individual categories shown in Fig. 2.1. Please note that 'news' (see Table 2.1) could be regarded as a distinct genre of website, but for simplicity it is absorbed into the 'Information' category. Similarly, 'entertainment' and 'education' are placed as subtypes of the 'services/products' genre.

The delivery of the various outcomes from the website can be achieved by electronic or terrestrial means (e.g., by a physical entity such as a CD, book, etc., that is purchased from the site, or a 'soft' entity such as software or electronically stored material).

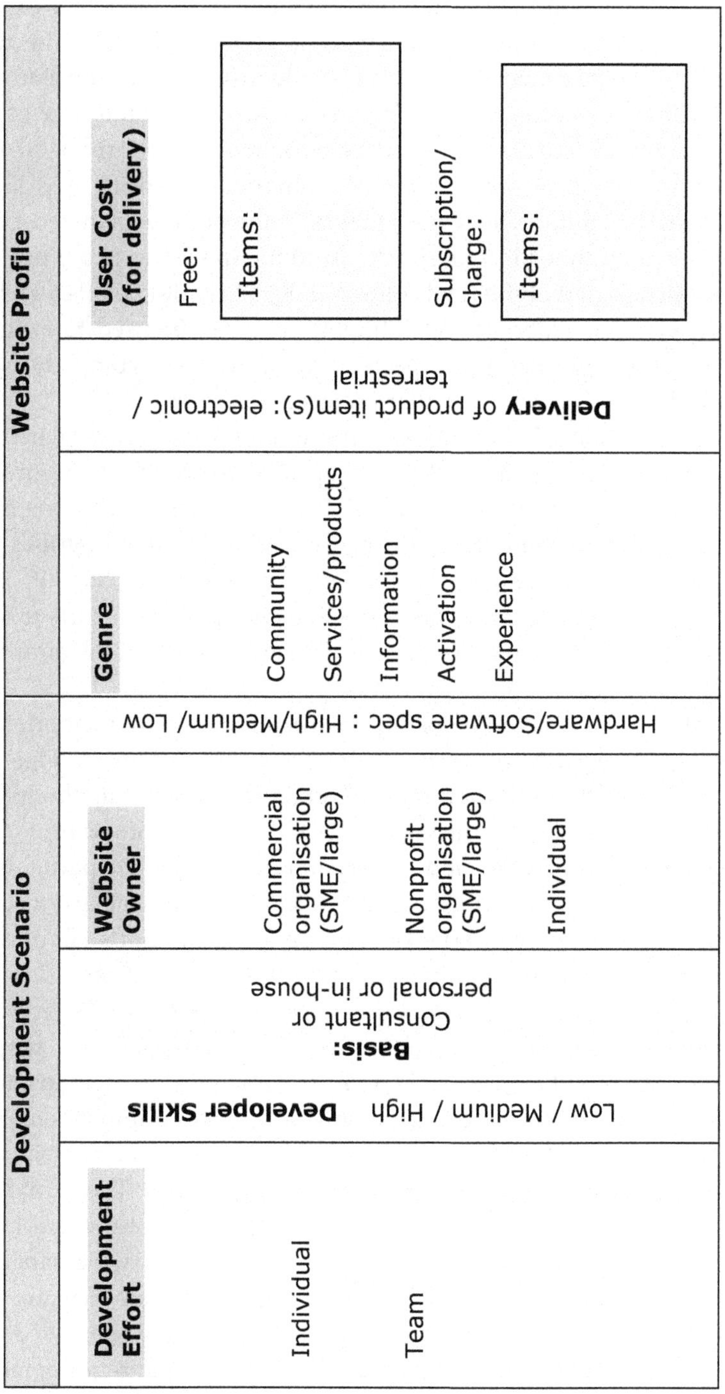

Fig. 2.1: Website design – technical context

Many websites will have a mixture of these types, and this can be indicated by stating an approximate percentage for each type. The final component of the framework (Fig. 2.1) is to identify the financial status of the 'transaction' – i.e., the items or materials received by the user of the website could be at zero direct cost or there could be some form of charge, either one-off costs or a subscription. For any given website, it is likely that there will be multiple deliverable items, some of these being cost-free but others having some kind of direct cost to the user. The two types can be summarised as part of the final column in Fig. 2.1, with details attached separately where appropriate. A highlighter pen can be used to indicate the nature of each of the other aspects in the chart – i.e., completing the scenario and profile for the particular project in question.

The identification of the various aspects of the project is a helpful starter to the designer (team), building up awareness about the project and its needs. There are numerous possible combinations of options from each of the columns, and the collective set of attributes describes the overall situation surrounding the website creation exercise. It is a starting point for gaining awareness of the 'bigger picture' for the project and provides a useful foundation for the detailed analysis of the aims and needs of the website.

The various advantages of using a structured design methodology generally apply equally to each of the scenarios shown in Fig. 2.1. However, the impact and importance of certain features of a methodology will vary according to the interests of each scenario. For example, the advantages of consistency and transparency might be particularly attractive to organisations and consultancies (i.e., this relates well to situations where there are a series of team projects) and not so important to individuals embarking on what might be their one and only website. Individuals who are not very experienced in website design and development might be very interested in easy-to-follow stepped approaches, whereas the more 'seasoned' implementers are perhaps quite familiar with the key steps typically involved in website implementation and perhaps more attracted by any new perspectives or innovations provided (e.g., as with BWD, on aesthetics and usability). Those that are developing a website for a client or for a set of people elsewhere in an organisation would probably look for the presence of a wide range of design documentation. This makes it easy to communicate designs and implementation ideas to them – for example, as a talking point to assist with the elicitation of important information, opinions, and requirements.

Website developers in any of the identified scenarios might be looking for a methodology that incorporates iterative cycles and formal stages where effectiveness and completeness are checked against ambitions. This might be especially relevant to those working on larger and more complex projects.

In each of the scenarios, it is important that all participants be very aware of the purpose behind a chosen methodology and very conversant with the steps and how they should be completed, individually and as a whole. The participants include developers, users, and clients. A short period of formal training may be necessary, especially if participants are not very experienced in the website development process. The training, which is best carried out in groups, would also help to build a good team spirit and identify or consolidate team player roles.

The broad nature of the site requirements will relate to the genre of the website, but the details of the design requirements will depend on the specific aims of the website in question. The details of those needs can only be ascertained after detailed analysis and consideration of the specific website aspirations. It is possible, however, to begin by forming a general view of what might be appropriate by further categorising website genres into typical 'subtypes' (this can be seen in Table 2.1) and highlighting typical features for the different genres (Table 2.2 shows some suggestions). The subtypes and features shown are examples and not exhaustive lists.

Each website genre and genre subtype will tend to have an element of content and purpose that overlaps with another genre, but the categories chosen can be based on whatever are the clear, predominant characteristics. Where there are clearly joint aims and aspirations of the website across more than one genre, we can describe that as a hybrid genre. Hence, items in more than one column in Table 2.1 could be highlighted.

Table 2.1: Website genre subtypes

Community	Services/Products	Information	Activation	Experience
locally based	retail	news	political	fantasy
social-based	consultancy	academic	cult	mystery
activity-based	education	press	conservation	arts
support	entertainment	promotion	sport	fun
interest	financial	interest	beliefs	religious
business	travel	career	arts	
	property	technical	vocation	
	item provision or creation	practical	career	
	skill/expertise	politics		

Table 2.2: Characteristic features for website genres

Community	Services/Products	Information	Activation	Experience
inviting	sales pitch	accurate	motivating	immersive
friendly	detailed	referenced	exciting	inspiring
sincere	professional	useful	make connection	aesthetically sensitive
supportive	direct	comprehensive	inspiring	exploratory
communicative	good scope	structured	interaction	adventure
no barriers	transaction enabled	indexed	steady/fast pace of change	
	efficient	clear		
	styled	further links		
	customer support	authoritative		

Although every site has its own set of unique aspirations and ambitions, it is the case that we can recognise 'overview level' attributes that can be assumed in most cases for sites of particular genres and subgenres. These typical features are indicated in Table 2.2. There could be a risk of relying too much on the generalisations, but it is useful to consider the trends when contemplating the effect of website genre on design.

The communities using the Internet are very wide-ranging in geographic, interest, technology, and experience terms. Figure 2.2 summarises the features and attributes that relate to the wide-ranging website community that might access a particular website. Making 'broad brushstroke' judgments regarding the likely age, web skills, mode of web use, and role of the target audience(s) for the website (hint: use a highlighter pen) helps formulate a profile that can be used as a reference in the design. Figure 2.2 includes other aspects, too, and knowledge about these also contributes to the overall awareness of suitable characteristics and features for the website. Although individual cases can be contradictory, experience tells us that there are trends that can be expected in terms of variations in design needs relating to variations in the data identified when studying Fig. 2.2, and these are illustrated in Figs. 2.3a and 2.3b. Some of the stated trends could be regarded as a little stereotypical but nonetheless provide useful guides. Initial testing and feedback from early prototype designs will provide confirmation and/or clarification.

Figures 2.2 and 2.3a/2.3b, and Tables 2.1 and 2.2, are to be used near the start of a project to get an initial indication of the main genre, environment, and user attributes, helping us get an understanding of general design considerations that relate to the project.

Websites – Implementation Process

The approach adopted for design and development of a website depends on several factors, including

- personal preferences and previous experiences of the developers/project leaders,
- if within a consultancy or development/client organisation, there might be in-house standards for developing information systems, including websites, and
- the time and cost budgets available for the project.

Age	Web Skills	Mode of Use	Role
Early School	Novice	Decisive	Professional
Teenager	Intermediate	Initial research	Student
Young Adult	Expert	Casual surfing	Customer
Adult		Specific	Employee
		General	Researcher
			Admirer
			Member

Male/female? Socio-economic status: world region:

Special needs (details or 'none'):

User's, technology level: high/med/low (connectionspeed/hardware/software)

Time Budget: urgent/contemplative/medium

Familiarity with topic/genre: low/med/high

Fig. 2.2: Website user characteristics

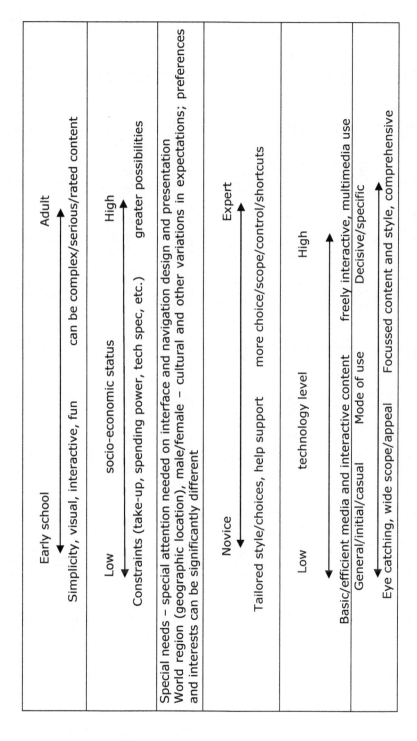

Fig. 2.3a: Website design feature trends (for user characteristics)

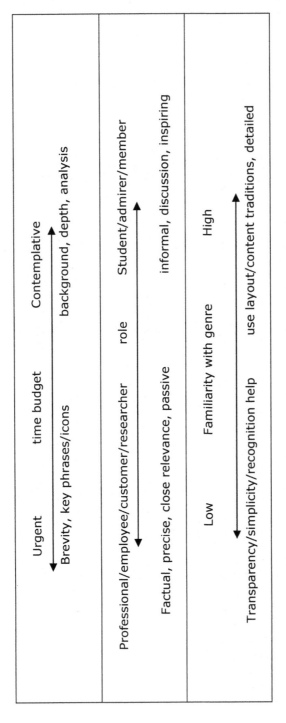

Fig. 2.3b: Website design feature trends (for user characteristics)

Clearly, the process described in this book (BWD) is our recommendation for any website design situation. However, there are many sources and examples of guidelines and approaches that are published and available (ranging from specific technical advice to broader, more comprehensive reference material). Some example references are given at the end of this chapter. Published guidelines tend to be centred around the traditional pattern of analysing requirements, discussing a user-centred design, and then implementation. The advice varies in its level of detail, comprehensiveness, and accessibility. Several sources have interesting hints and tips for good website design and project management. The process described in this book can absorb the details of guidelines selected from elsewhere (e.g., [2–5]) and/or favoured detailed good practice from any previous projects. The designer is not forced into using a strict list of techniques and software for each technical task – as it is the concept and principle of each BWD step that is important – and so integration with existing skills is straightforward and very acceptable.

The essence of the process for a website design and implementation project is as follows:

1. Understand/specify what is needed from and with the website.
2. Ascertain and acquire budgets for time, skills, and the software/ hardware needed.
3. Identify and procure the content needed for the website – text, pictures, video, sound, animations, graphics, etc.
4. Design layouts and structures (navigation movement, content organisation, screen layouts, website structure and style, etc.).
5. Digitise and edit/process the content material (including compression of media files).
6. Prototype and build the webpages (iterative with evaluation).
7. Transfer all files to webserver hardware (and purchase webserver disc space if not already available).
8. Test and evaluate the website online. Make changes and enhancements as necessary.
9. Utilise an existing Internet domain name (the address used by web users to access your website) or purchase one.
10. Promote the website (traditional advertising, links on other websites, email to lists, register keywords/links on web search engine websites).

This book deals directly with supporting the completion of all these aspects. The details of the BWD methodology and how to use it to create an effective website are given in Section 2 of this book. Ahead of embarking on such a project, however, there are certain skills and preparations that must be put into place.

Preparation Ahead of a BWD Project

The activity of developing effective websites is one that requires substantial effort and skill. Using a methodology such as BWD does not replace those ingredients, but a methodology does support the process and maximise the effectiveness of the outcomes. So, certain skills and personal characteristics must be in place (within the individual or across the team, depending on the size of the project) as important starting points for a website project. Some of these tasks/skills could be contracted out if not readily available otherwise. They include the following:

Technical/task skills
- Requirements analysis and specification design
- HTML/DHTML programming and/or experience with DHTML-generating packages – e.g., Dreamweaver, FrontPage, etc.; alternatively, a website can be created using 'non-DHTML' software such as Flash (Macromedia)
- Graphics – e.g., editing/processing images
- Word processing/writing for the Web
- Content selection and acquisition
- Content creation/production and presentation
- Layout design
- Usability – heuristics, evaluation, design
- Aesthetics – awareness, evaluation, ideas
- Audio/video – creation, capture, editing, encoding, streaming
- Animation/multimedia packages – e.g., Flash
- Streaming – e.g., RealMedia
- Website server hosting and full acceptance testing
- Management of the website – 'post-implementation'

The main personal characteristics/skills that are necessary across website development teams are as follows:

- Communication
- Interviewing/research
- Leadership
- Teamwork
- Innovativeness
- Stamina and perseverance
- Self-reliance
- Creativity
- Logic
- Analytical skills
- Pragmatism
- Diplomacy
- Project and team management

These skills and characteristics can be gained through specialist training, personal development, and/or by selective recruitment for a particular project. Depending on the nature and size of the project itself, the prioritisation of the items in the lists above will vary, so preparation and selection of resources clearly needs to take this into account.

If preparing for quite a sensitive and/or important website development project it might be useful to build up the necessary skills in advance of a project by working on a case study or smaller websites in the required genre. This tends to be more effective than, for example, training using separate isolated tasks and exercises.

Projects need to make choices of software packages and hardware platforms to be used during the development process. This will be partly governed by your previous experience and existing technology availability and further by special demands of the project and the budget available. DHTML-generating packages (e.g., Macromedia Dreamweaver, Microsoft Frontpage, etc.) and multimedia packages have learning curves, so early decisions on this aspect are needed. There are also lead times to contend with if hardware and software have to be purchased and installed.

The success of a website design and implementation project ultimately depends on the abilities of the people involved and the resources and time made available to them. A good methodology alone is not enough. In addition to the wider technical and personal skills listed above, it is necessary to be conversant and comfortable with the methodology process to be adopted. There are a series of exercises (seminar, tutorial, and case study) placed at numerous strategic points in this book. They are designed to progressively contribute to good preparation. Students and tutors are expected to make use of the seminar and tutorial questions and integrate these into their course of study as appropriate. However, this book is aimed at industry professionals, too, and depending on experience and particular interests, these exercises might be useful.

For the case study exercises, it is recommended to use a small project as a basis, perhaps a hypothetical one, with realistic parameters, but it can also be a real project. If it is essential to begin work on a 'key' project immediately, then this would be possible, too, by going through each chapter and applying, each set of case study exercises included in the chapter.

In certain situations (for example, where teams are large and/or preparation time needs to be accelerated), it might be necessary to adopt specialist training in BWD.

Chapter Exercises

Seminar Topics

1. The role of the website user might be that of a student, researcher, professional, etc. Why is it important to consider this when designing a website?
2. Identify any website genres that could be added to those listed in this chapter (Table 2.1). Discuss the justification for any candidate additions.
3. Discuss whether it might be the case that for some genres, and perhaps some user types, website design could be easier than for others.

Tutorial Exercises

1. State three examples of 'user roles' when accessing a website, and consider the variety of 'modes of use' for each of those roles.
2. Name one 'attraction' of the BWD website design methodology relevant to each of (a) a novice developer, (b) an experienced developer, and (c) a project manager for several projects.
3. List five key skills (technical and personal) that are typically needed to prepare for a website design project.

Case Study

1. Identify which 'development scenario' and 'website profile' (use Fig. 2.1) fits your own case study situation.
2. Make a checklist of tasks and activities that you (personally) need to complete as preparation before commencing with BWD itself.
3. Build up a summary picture of the target user audience for your case study website by noting their anticipated profile(s) (based on Fig. 2.2) and associated generalised features, as indicated in Figs. 2.3a/b.

Chapter References

1. Badre A. (2002), *Shaping Web Usability: Interaction Design in Context*, Addison-Wesley, Reading, MA.
2. Cato J. (2001), *User Centred Web Design*, Addison-Wesley, Reading, MA.
3. Concepcion A. (2002), *Professional Website Design from Start to Finish,* F&W Publications.
4. Krug S. (2000), Don't Make Me Think, New Riders, Indianapolis ISBN: 0-7897-2310-7
5. Knuckles C.D. & Yuen D.S. (2004), *Web Applications: Concepts and Real World Design*, Wiley, New York.

CHAPTER THREE

Website Usability

Overview

This chapter reflects on a topic that has roots in a long history of general information systems software interface design work and in recent years has gained a new focus – in the context of website design. The topic is (website) usability.

We look at what the main website usability experts are saying and put this into the context of a structured website design methodology.

Give and Gain

If you give time to this chapter (55 minutes or so, plus time for the exercises), this is what you will gain:

- knowledge of widely recognised (and enhanced) guidelines for achieving good web usability;

- an appreciation of a set of heuristics that can be applied to website design;
- awareness of how web usability needs can differ;
- an introduction to the concept of 'straight' and 'curved' usability.

What Is Usability?

We all know what usability is … or maybe rather what poor usability is! (Just think of most video recorders and the time we have spent crawling on the floor puzzling over how to set the timer!)

Good usability is when we use something almost or completely without noticing that we are using an interface to do the thing we want to do (e.g., boxes of fruit juice with those nice plastic lids). If we do notice the interface, it might be to register the pleasure of using that interface. Poor usability is when we get frustrated and the method/interface seems to be a barrier, stopping us from making progress (e.g., a friend gives you a lift in their car, which is unfamiliar to you, and then you have to open the door to get out, almost always a problem to do quickly and effectively).

Now, these two examples were chosen deliberately to represent practical objects that we use as everyday items – as the characteristics of 'usability' apply to almost everything. This includes software and websites.

Regardless of the target item, when we are rating usability (or designing for good usability), we should consider the following general aspects:

- Could anyone (i.e., any member of the target user population) use the item for the intended purpose?
- Could they use it with ease?
- Does it slow the (main) activity down, or does it adversely affect it in another way?
- Does the 'usability approach' contribute positively to the (main) purpose in some way?

These are general features of usability and hence apply to website usability just as much as to, say, the design of a kettle or a fan heater, for example.

Nielsen and Molich [8] summarise good website usability as being easy to learn, easy to remember, effective to use, understandable, and giving satisfaction. Jeffrey Rubin [10] states that there are four key factors in usability: usefulness, effectiveness, learnability, and attitude.

Usability is not really a strange 'mystic' subject that is complicated or 'remote'. It is something that we live with and work with all of the time – we just might think of it as something else (perhaps convenience, quality, or straightforwardness). In fact, Steve Krug describes usability as definitely not 'rocket surgery' ™ and that it is very much based on common sense [1]. On the other hand, there is such a large community of consultants and academics researching and working with an ongoing quest to grasp the Holy Grail of this topic that it can't be that easy! There are lots of books, conferences, newsgroups, and other communities dedicated to the single subject of 'usability'. This is a good indication of its importance, the depth and breadth of the issues involved, and the general interest in the subject. In this book, we give our perspective on designing for website usability and derive a set of guidelines plus a set of heuristics using established published work as a starting point.

Although this chapter presents a list of recommended guidelines, let's also note that the battle to achieve good, 'guaranteed' software interface design has not yet been won – in any software implementations, let alone website implementations (even though there have been many steps of progress). In other words, there is not yet a universally accepted set of rules to follow to ensure good usability. The task and nature of usability are too complex (partly because of software use being human-centred) for that to be the case.

This chapter does not give all the answers about what precisely to include in a website design to achieve maximum usability – there are way too many variables and influences involved to do that. Also, even for a specific website scenario, the exact features of good usability design can (and maybe should) be a very personal thing. Your own thought, passion, and patience are needed to explore the possibilities, evaluate ideas, and strive to achieve the design aspirations. There are a variety of possible good usability designs for given situations.

Aesthetics also have a bearing here – two different good usability designs might have entirely different aesthetics, and consideration of this would have an impact on which usability design idea is chosen. The usability features of a website directly influence the aesthetic character-stics. These two aspects are intertwined and have to be considered in parallel when designing a website. Chapter 4 discusses our analysis of aesthetics.

In the design documentation adopted as part of the website design process described in this book, a form is included that the designer uses to document the usability requirements and design. This comment might alert you to two things:

1. The process (described in full in Section 2, Chapters 5–8) helps by using documentation to identify and communicate the principles and reasoning of the design (including usability) to yourself, your team, and your clients.

2. 'Usability needs' vary and design solutions are different for each website project. The needs depend largely on the genre of the site, its audience, and the aims of the site. For example, a 'philosophical' site may wish you to experience some chosen lines of thought or analysis as part of using the site, as well as the content itself. Other sites might be required or hope to be entertaining or challenging, for example, in the process of using the site. Sites that are in the business of selling products may be more interested in usability that has an emphasis on transparency and speed. Each of these examples makes particular demands on the usability design, requiring differing and sometimes unique design ideas to achieve the desired usability features.

Before going deeper into the task of website usability design, let's explore a parallel with a practical task that we all experience at some time or another – 'getting our home decor right'. The task of designing and implementing our 'home decor' is similar to (software) usability design (and, in particular, website usability design) in lots of ways:

*   For a start, it's easy to add paint and paper, put tiles down, and put tiles up, but painful and costly to change it later if it doesn't work (vis à vis creating webpages and webpage items, and costly amendments if applied later)!
*   It's easy to *do* something, but lots of care and thought are needed to get the right result.
*   Friends and neighbours almost certainly won't think it is as good as you do (and might ask, "Is it finished yet?"). This compares closely with websites in that other developers and

viewers are likely to have a reaction different from what you would expect.

- You will probably enjoy the experimentation with paints, etc., more than actually looking at it later! Similarly, designing and making websites can be fun as a process in itself.
- Lots of different results can be achieved with more or less the same materials.
- Visitors might not notice the detail of what you do but do notice the overall effect.
- The purpose, usability, and aesthetics are all important aspects, and they interrelate.

How do we tackle the task of designing the decor? Probably for a start we look around at what we would regard as good examples of what we are trying to achieve. We might gain some technical and styling knowledge (from books, TV programmes, part-time courses perhaps). At this point, we would reexamine the budget. To decide whether to 'buy skills in' (pay for someone else to do it) or perhaps readjust our plans (either downgrading our previously ambitious ideas or deciding to increase the budget to allow us to do that 'little bit extra'!). One thing that we certainly would not do is to start the job without knowing (and liking) what we are trying to create. The cost in time, materials, and gathering and obtaining the material content, plus the pain of living with something that doesn't 'work' or 'satisfy', would be too great a burden to bear.

The same applies to website making – i.e., we design first, working closely with the motivations and deliverable desires driving the design, before committing too much in costly materials, time, and entrenched implementations.

Designing for Good Usability

There have been many hours and years of research into, and practical experience of, software usability design and evaluation. Notable explorers and exponents of website usability include Jacob Nielsen [2], Steve Krug [1], and Jared Spool [5]. Web usability research, and practice, benefits from several years of HCI (human–computer interaction) research prior to and since the inception of the Web. Websites are quite a special instance of information system (IS) software, usually with complex non-hierarchical pathways potentially to be followed, together with the presence of a growing intensity of multimedia content, and each webpage and website has multifarious competing pages/sites that are literally one or two clicks away at any one time. This quite severely distorts the traditional levels of user tolerance and expectations that can be relied upon by the developer. The user also tends to be using the Web on a personal basis and not acting as an employee or team member, so there are no 'organisational' rules and constraints or financial issues (zero 'cost' of surfing to another site) to sway the choice of the user to perhaps persevere with an application (in this case, a website). That is, traditionally users of IS software have, or do, become locked into using a particular package (due to the hassle of moving to another environment), but for website users it is so easy and quick to go elsewhere (to another site) if not satisfied fairly quickly.

In addition to relating the usability characteristics of a website to the specific purpose targets, it is also necessary to keep a close eye on the desired aesthetic of the website. Usability design and aesthetic design are closely related – changes in one will often impact and alter the characteristics and attributes of the other. Earlier, we noted that Nielsen and Molich [8] refer to the component of satisfaction in terms of usability. This is an indication of the connection between usability and aesthetics. We look at the relationship between them in a little more detail in the next chapter (Chapter 4).

To achieve good usability, the starting point is to be clear on the ambitions and desires of the site itself. The nature and purpose of the site will have an influence on the style and detail of the usability features. In possibly the majority of cases, we will wish to make the access to and navigation around parts of the site as smooth and intuitive as possible – i.e., self-evident (this could be described as 'straight' usability). In some cases, however, website designers may be looking for a usability that is a little more abstract, intriguing, and/or challenging (we would describe this as 'curved usability'). In all cases, however, it is our task as designers to recognise the ideal usability characteristics and design the site to target those ideals. We also need to give thorough attention to the needs, expectations, and characteristics of the targeted users and also to the context(s) of the website's usage.

The next part of this chapter is split into two sections so that we can fully consider both straight usability and curved usability in detail. We discuss a detailed list of guidelines and conclude with a derived set of usability heuristics. The final section of the chapter deals briefly with aspects such as the consideration of target user characteristics, context of use, and usability testing.

Straight Usability

Typical examples of sites that require 'self-evident' (straight) usability characteristics might be a solicitor's website, an insurance company's website, or a standard retail website.

Two examples of websites that could be regarded as 'straight' usability type websites, shown in Figs. 3.1a [see plate 12] and 3.1b, illustrate a typical online retail website and a legal services website. The retail website has a clear array of pictures and supporting text, with attention-grabbing advert areas on the screen. The navigation to obtain further information and progress to make a purchase is also quite clear. It has neat layout with a focus on keeping attention, avoiding any confusion or delay, and making a sale.

Fig. 3.1a: Curry's retail site (UK)   Fig. 3.1b: Solicitor's portal site

The legal services website also reflects a simple 'straight' usability style but has a slightly different aesthetic style, according to differing target characteristics of the website.

A book that is nicely to the point and relates particularly to achieving good usability for this type of website is Don't Make Me Think by Steve Krug [1]. It would be a significant achievement to design a usable interface and navigation scheme that is so obvious that the user doesn't need to 'consciously' think about what to do to gain access to the right place. Krug [1] explains that self-evident design is achieved by a simplicity approach (but not necessarily simplistic), with great care taken to choose words, graphics, and layouts that do not confuse and that strike a familiar chord with the user of the website.

Figure 3.2 shows a list of points to guide you when developing your 'straight usability' website designs. These guidelines (Fig. 3.2) and a set of heuristics that are described later (Figs. 3.5a/3.5b) are developed as rationalisations of ideas previously introduced by Jacob Nielsen [2]. The heuristics also absorb salient aspects of the ideas put forward by Muller et al. [3] (which were introduced at that time to enhance coverage of 'user process orientation'). The development of the ideas benefits from reading the work of Steve Krug [1], Jared Spool [5], and John Cato [4], amongst others in this area.

The 'straight usability' guidelines are split into four sections, grouping them into those that relate to

- Content assimilation – the nature of understanding (or otherwise) of what is available and presented on the webages;
- Navigation – the ease with which the website user is comfortable with and clear about the website structure and locating items of interest;
- Audience awareness – considerations of the human elements of website design and use (the demands, interactions, and idiosyncrasies);
- Process – a focus here on the importance of testing and planning for usability as part of the wider project approach.

The guidelines, grouped into subsections for clarity, are for use in tackling the task of recognising the design needs for your website and producing design ideas for those needs. The recommendation is to consider these categorised guidelines when designing the usability characteristics of a project website and in conjunction with the genre-based website characteristics presented in Chapter 2. In Chapter 2, we looked at types of websites and website user characteristics – in particular in Table 2.1 and in Fig. 2.2. That analysis can help us in establishing the usability characteristics we wish to target in our websites.

The cultural aspect also needs to be considered. Barber and Badre [7] have researched this and found that existing sites are now beginning to follow styles that have particular relevance to the culture of the main targeted audience. For example, this concerns the orientation of text (left to right or right to left), colour combinations (e.g., to match national flag colours), and the use of national emblems, flags, or other icons.

Content assimilation

1. Simplicity in design is often very successful.
2. Brevity and clarity are like gold dust.
3. Website content is *glanced at,* not carefully and slowly studied and read.
4. Webpage choices (links/selections) should be designed with speed and impatience in mind.

Navigation

5. Comfortable (easy choices and recognition) and speedy navigation around the site is desirable.
6. Well-chosen (unambiguous, brief, relevant, true) words and an understandable layout of visuals and text are particularly vital.
7. Presenting a complete view of the site and current location at any time the user is moving around the site is a key navigation component.
8. Clear navigation is *at least* as important as the content material.
9. The 'virtual' world of a website suffers in navigation terms unless landmarks can be 'planted' in some way and represent the 'bigger picture'.

Audience awareness

10. The homepage is special. It's the shop window, the front page – everyone and everything wants to be in on it.
11. Keep the site fresh, accurate, and relevant, and react promptly to any invited (audience) interaction.
12. Web users are fantastically varied, with unique reactions and characteristics, so audience identi-fication and analysis helps, but designs have to cater for complex human nature. The role and situation can affect user reactions.
13. Users are not obliged to care about or like our websites; *we* must trigger/nurture that attraction.
14. Good (usable) webpages are like good road signs and good billboard adverts; looking at how *they* work is worthwhile research.

Process

15. Testing (including user testing) for usability is extremely important – start this early in the project.
16. Planning, design, and an iterative process are very important features in any approach.

Fig. 3.2: 'Straight usability guidelines' (design hints)

We need to take this into account in our usability and aesthetic designs for our websites. Ideally, the designer forms a clear definition of the target usability characteristics that follow the general guidelines, are related to the genre expectations and traditions, and also represent ideas and plans that are unique to the aspirations of the particular website being designed. We have mentioned 'curved' usability, and it is possible that your project website would fit this usability type rather than the 'straight' type. If so, then the usability guidelines to be followed need to have some differences from those given in Fig. 3.2 to take into account the adjustment in perspective.

Curved Usability

'Curved usability' is a new term that is introduced in this book simply to help us distinguish between 'ordinary' usability needs (i.e., similar to those that might be associated with traditional business software information systems) and the quite different usability requirements demanded by certain genres of websites. The term 'curved usability' is used in the context of web usability, as it is specifically the Web that offers a powerful and fairly distinct split between 'business-like, serious, corporate, and information resource' type material and that of a more esoteric nature (e.g., 'fun', artistic, thought provoking, cult, etc.).

This suggests the need for two main categories of usability approaches – straight usability, and curved usability. A curved usability approach provides a different dimension to allow for the special demands of addressing the needs of these 'esoteric' type website designs.

Why use the word 'curved'? It reminds us that we may need to bend some of the 'traditional' usability rules and that (rather like drawing curved lines) curved usability can be more challenging to map between perceived needs and actual implementation.

Typical 'curved' usability websites are those for fine arts, game/role playing, entertainment by puzzles/mystery, cult film/music, etc. The example screenshot shown in Fig. 3.3a [see plate 13] illustrates a typical artist's website, although sites on this topic can be much more abstract in their navigation and clarity of purpose. The links to facilities to make contact, make purchases, and obtain further information, etc., exist on the page but are not blatant and do not detract from the main focus – the artist's work.

A certain degree of time and exploration is needed to find out which icon is for which purpose.

Fig. 3.3a: An artist's website   Fig. 3.3b: A musician's website

Another example of a curved usability website is illustrated in Fig. 3.3b [see plate 13], which is a musician's website and has a very interesting and obscure interface – the intrigue of which is intended to reflect the style and scope of music created by the website owner. The artwork is all original and hand-drawn, and the changes due to mouse cursor position and clicking are interesting and sometimes surprising or humorous. Some changes appear without user intervention. The aesthetic and usability designs suit the experimental approach of the owner and content of the website.

To achieve this type of curved usability design, it is useful to have an amended list of usability guidelines and heuristics. The guidelines in Figs. 3.4a and 3.4b are an extension of those in Fig. 3.2 and again are divided into the four areas of content assimilation, navigation, audience awareness, and process.

It is the first two categories that need a new perspective of attention if the website is thought to be of the curved variety. The content assimilation and navigation sections therefore have a special set of notes that relate to curved usability. Hence, the details of the website design that have impacts on the usability characteristics of the site should be formed with consideration of these new perspectives.

		Straight Usability	Curved Usability
Content Assimilation	1	Simplicity in design is often very successful.	The target impact and experience of the website might be one of obscurity, abstractedness, challenge, intrigue, and/or chance. The 'traditional' notion of simple, clear, and speedily understood designs could be replaced by one catering for whatever 'curved usability' impact and experience is desired.
	2	Brevity and clarity are like gold dust.	
	3	Website content is *glanced at*, not carefully and slowly studied and read.	
	4	Choices (links/selections) available to website users should be designed with speed and impatience in mind.	
Navigation	5	Comfortable (easy choices and recognition) and speedy navigation around the website is desirable.	Navigation ease and awareness of position within the total map of the site might be things that need to be made 'less comfortable', not quite so 'immediate', and perhaps more 'conceptual' to match the desired website style and character.
	6	Well-chosen (unambiguous, brief, relevant, true) words and an understandable layout of visuals and text are particularly vital.	
	7	Presenting a complete view of a site and the current location in the site at any time the user is moving around the site is a key navigation component.	
	8	Clear navigation is *at least* as important as the content material.	
	9	Navigation in the 'virtual' world of the website suffers unless landmarks are planted in some way to represent the 'bigger picture'.	

Fig. 3.4a: Straight and curved website usability guidelines

		Straight and Curved Usability
Audience Awareness	10	Homepages are special and especially difficult! It's the shop window, the front page, the opening scene in a film, the news headlines, the front cover, the first impression, the 'sink or swim' page, and like a life raft everyone and everything wants to be in on it and be in prime position!
	11	Keep the site fresh, accurate, relevant, and up-to-date, and react promptly to any invited (audience) interaction
	12	Web users are fantastically varied, with unique reactions and characteristics, so audience identification and analysis helps, but designs have to cater for complex human nature. The role and situation can affect user reactions.
	13	Users are not obliged to care about or like our websites; *we* have to trigger and nurture that attraction.
	14	Good (usable) webpages are like good road signs and good billboard adverts, so looking at how *they* work is worthwhile research.
Process	15	Testing (including one or more cycles of user testing) for usability is extremely important – start this early in the project.
	16	Planning, design, and an iterative process are very important features in any approach.

Fig. 3.4b: Straight and curved website usability guidelines

For a particular website, the designer would need to identify a reasonable level of detail regarding usability characteristics before the design detail could be derived. The suggested process approach to be taken to achieve this is described later in the book (Chapters 5–8).

The broad categorisation into straight and curved types serves to draw attention to something often missed in website design discussions – that website usability needs are not universal. There is no one set of rules and guidance that applies to all situations and sites. Each of the two broad categories could conceivably be split down again to subcategories, but that is probably not that useful for the purposes of designing our websites. The main thing is to recognise whether the site is of the straight or curved variety (as this will heighten the awareness of the usability needs applicable to your website), and then build up a specific usability profile that would be particularly relevant and appropriate for that specific website. A unique and appropriate usability identity is the aim. Incidentally, to work on the desired aesthetics in conjunction with usability is advisable – more on aesthetics in Chapter 4.

Each website has a different combination of usability and aesthetic requirements, depending on the exact nature and purpose of the website, and the consequences of not addressing each of these requirements carefully and comprehensively can be catastrophic to the success of a website. It is this, to an extent, that sets website design apart from the demands of general software interface design.

In website design, we have the task of achieving optimal usability alongside creating an appropriate and effective aesthetic and alongside making sure that the website design fulfils the targeted purpose(s) of the website. The combined focus on website aesthetics and usability is increasingly regarded as important in website design [6]. So, in our website design work, we need to coordinate the usability design thinking with the consideration of aesthetics and website purpose. For example, when working on improving usability, changes in the details of our website design might also affect the aesthetic and might also impact how well the targeted purpose characteristics of the website are satisfied. A similar situation arises when working on improving the aesthetic by making adjustments to the website design. Adding or changing purpose charac- teristics could also affect usability and/or aesthetic attributes.

To simplify the management of these 'interrelationship' impacts, BWD begins the design work by establishing the purpose design needs. In the light of this information, the tasks of establishing the usability and the aesthetic design requirements are carried out jointly (as part of the same step of the BWD process). Towards the end of the project life cycle, all three aspects (usability, aesthetics, and purpose) are tested together in the same project step (Step 11).

Heuristics

Usability heuristics can be regarded as 'rules of thumb' notions that can be used as a basis for usability evaluation of a design. The suggestions made in Figs. 3.5a and 3.5b are developed as rationalisations of ideas pre- viously introduced by Jacob Nielsen [2].

Heuristic A: Awareness and Control

Straight

User needs to have clear awareness about what is happening at any one time (Is something being processed? Is something closing/opening? etc.), as simple as being sure the user *notices* that their previous request/selection has been processed. Consistency is as important as clarity; clutter is as problematic as poor content. Closely associated is the notion that the user should always feel comfortably in control of the situation – knowing where they are in the site, knowing what options and possibilities lie before them (and how to trigger them), including how to easily 'undo' to 'get back on track'.

Curved

Ownership of control and the degree of user awareness are not fixed, varying according to the virtual location of the user and the experience aspirations (of site and user). Escape routes and options to refresh/reset to be considered – and often implemented. The detailed characteristics and features of mystery, suspense, surprise, suspended reality, craziness, etc., must have strong foundations in the site/purpose aims. It should be reasonably evident to the casual visitor to the site how to escape the experience if they so wish.

Heuristic B: Wavelength and Aesthetics

The words, the language (textual and visual), and the style all need to make a *connection* with the targeted audience and connect their interest and intentions to the purpose and possibilities of the website. In short, the website design needs to be on the right 'wavelength' – achieving the ideal aesthetics of the site. This may entail tapping into the right emotions and cultural and aspirational energies and latching onto the 'real world' and web icons and traditions. Presentation, visual/media content, expectations, intentions and identity, flow, and impression are all important.

Heuristic C: Care and Reason

The site's interface, layout, and functionality design should 'ooze' careful and reasoned thought by the designer. Everything should have a place, be in the right place, and clearly be the best and most appropriate. Vacuum cleaners that have automated cable-coiling, cars that have drink holders, and shirts that have spare buttons all have that 'extra edge' over similar products that just do the minimum.

Fig. 3.5a: Straight and curved website usability heuristics (for design evaluation)

Heuristic D: Efficiency and Help
Straight The design should make it speedy and uncomplicated to make choices and trigger events. Extra online help (including wizards) could for example be made available when needed (with the user *choosing* when it is needed!), and fast-track elements to the design could also be considered for 'expert' users (but not be noticeable by other users).
Curved In extreme 'curved' cases, this heuristic becomes irrelevant and redundant – as the level of speed and complexity has to be placed in the context of the intended nature of the website. Online help could be useful, but its presence may often be in conflict with the site ambitions.

Fig. 3.5b: Straight and curved website usability heuristics (for design evaluation)

The heuristics also absorb salient aspects of the ideas put forward by Muller et al. [3] (which were introduced at that time to enhance coverage of 'user process orientation'). The four heuristics are for use in assessing the website usability once a prototype or finished website has been completed.

'Awareness and control' relates to a user's awareness of what is happening (e.g., processing/action) and the feeling of being in control over the processing when using the website and in control over how to access and initiate whatever functionality is desired.

To successfully address the 'wavelength and aesthetic' aspect is to make a clear and positive connection with the target audience in terms of how the purpose(s) of the website are provided with good and appropriate usability characteristics. The usability design should also be effective in terms of style and 'feel' (relate to aesthetic characteristics).

The third heuristic is 'care and reason'. The usability design should make the clear impression that there has been careful and reasoned effort put into that design. This means that every detail requires thorough attention. The final heuristic ('efficiency and help') deals with technical performance and help offered to users if and when usability problems arise.

Figures 3.5a and 3.5b illustrate how the use of the heuristics can differ between 'straight' and 'curved' usability situations.

Project Usage

Chapters 5–8 describe and explain in detail a process recommended for use as a structured website design methodology. Within that process, it is necessary to specify thoughtful usability needs for a project and design for those usability needs.

The sixteen guideline items given in Figs. 3.4a and 3.4b should serve as a checklist – a set of general aspects that need to be considered and achieved. The details of exactly how your design satisfies those generalised aspects will depend on two main things – your design imagination and the fine details of the usability needs that you identify in the early analysis (of requirements) stage of the process. Those design details cannot be predicted here and furthermore need to be relevant and unique to each website. To attempt to identify and use a reference set of solutions suggests the thought of many sites being 'cloned' from one such set of ideas. This has the obvious potential drawback that the site will lack unique innovation and creativity.

The four heuristics are for us to use after initial and final prototype designs have been implemented to help assess and evaluate the general usability design of the website. In addition, there will be those specific detailed usability needs that you will have identified earlier in the BWD process (which will need to be specifically tested). The guidelines/ heuristics suggested should be utilised in your project as described above for straight usability or for curved usability. The versions you use will depend on whether you perceive the general usability needs of your project website as straight or curved.

Target Users and Context of Use

The guidelines and heuristics described in the previous sections make some references to user needs and expectations – key aspects to consider alongside your ambitions for the site as an owner and developer. Making a distinct effort to get to know and understand the preferences, background, and interests of your site's main target audiences is clearly going to be helpful in terms of designing for good usability and designing an effective website in every sense.

To consider the context of use might not be quite so obviously important at first. However, the same website can be used by the same user in different contexts, some of which can make the website become totally unusable unless pre-empted. The following are typical examples of contexts within which websites might be used:

- Hardware/software – shared workstation, personalised workstation setup, low/high specification, physical constraints (e.g., for easily using a keyboard/mouse), unusual input device (e.g., touch screen).
- Atmosphere – relaxed, rushed, quiet, interruptive, home, office, private, public, noisy.
- Tasking – single, multiple, constant, varying, infrequent, regular.
- Experience – first-time user, expert (specific or general).
- Intensity of purpose – leisure, hobby/fun, professional, business, study/training.

In Chapter 2, there are illustrations of how website genres and website user types can be categorised and how the various categorisations can be related to features of the websites designed for use in those contexts (Tables 2.1 and 2.2 and Figs. 2.2, 2.3a, and 2.3b). So, for the same site purpose (from a developer/owner point of view), the usability of the site might require special design considerations depending on the demands of the particular contexts of use – of the individuals and, in particular, circumstances of using the site. The practicalities of predicting or recognising the context and then providing designs that optimise suitability in that context are not simple but have to be considered. There could be different versions of the website, or designs could target 'average' or likely situations, and all versions have to be tested (including with target users) to verify the effectiveness of the designs.

Usability Testing

In testing, lots of thought and 'soul searching' by developers and clients is absolutely vital. Prototyping and testing/evolving ideas along the way is a very useful project approach, too. Usability can be imagined, planned, and designed, but most of all it has to be tested.

The timing of usability tests is important – the optimum is to test early (in the project) and at least twice in detail (with real people) before going 'live' with the site. Time is needed to be able to react to feedback and realisations identified during testing.

It is generally not very effective to use 'focus groups' for testing – i.e., to the exclusion of 'traditional' testing (as it can be misleading and costly). Use them, though (say, 4–8 person discussion groups, and early in the project), to discuss the general thrust and nature of a site using the dynamics of a group discussion to produce a picture of how users in general are likely to react to the site.

For the usability testing, individual users are needed to get feedback on how well the site actually works. They can be asked to explore the site and try to work out what it is for and what it can provide (and how), or they can be asked to complete specific tasks. In the main BWD testing step (Step 11), all three of the main attributes of website design (usability, aesthetics, and purpose) are examined. The characteristics of the implemented design are checked against the detailed requirements as established and documented earlier in BWD.

Testers should be new to the website and also not connected with the development team in any way (to reduce the potentially distorting effects of familiarity and internal politics). Try not to rely on usability testing for *selecting* designs – the feedback at best will *contribute* to your decision making (by providing good information). Test feedback can be captured in several ways: questionnaires, note taking, discussions, and session video recording are all good for detailed analysis, and having a person to facilitate the session (to help generate a commentary/dialogue) is essential. Summary results (including action to be taken) should be recorded, where the effectiveness of specific design features targeted is checked.

In Perfetti [9], it is stated that Rolf Molich advises that usability reports must themselves be usable by making them short, by including summary sections, by including positive points as well as negative ones, and by classifying comments (prioritised by importance). The BWD usability test documentation (like the other BWD test documentation) is designed to support these notions.

Summary

This chapter has discussed website usability combining knowledge, information, and guidelines based on academic research plus industry practice and experience. A website that has 'good' usability is where one can understand, use, and navigate around the site in a suitable manner. The best approach to achieve the desired level of usability is to utilise a usability design approach that is 'user-centred' and to conduct usability testing as part of the development process (and early in the project cycle).

The chapter introduces the notions of straight usability and curved usability – catering for two identified broad categories of websites. Comprehensive sets of guidelines for straight and curved usability are provided to help you work towards achieving good website usability results. A refined and enhanced set of usability heuristics is also presented. The issues of usability testing, target user characteristics, and the context(s) within which the site is to be used are also discussed. We revisit usability as part of working through the BWD methodology in Chapters 5–8.

Chapter Exercises

Seminar Topics

1. Discuss the differences and overlaps between *straight* and *curved* usability.
2. To what extent can usability testing truly measure website usability?
3. Discuss how usability designs and changes to these designs might affect aesthetic characteristics of a website.

Tutorial Exercises

1. Briefly describe four heuristics that can be used in assessing and designing for website usability (distinguishing between *straight* and *curved* usability needs).
2. List three examples of existing websites that have a need for straight and three for curved usability features. (To answer this question, you might need to surf the Web.)
3. How well do you think the sites you have listed in previous question achieve the desired usability characteristics? Make suggestions for any design changes for usability improvement.

Case Study

1. Write one or more paragraphs describing the usability characteristics ideally targeted for your case study site.
2. Decide whether your case study website would be regarded as a straight usability or curved usability site.
3. Write out general guidelines for the usability testing stages of development of your website – main aspects to be tested and the criteria for evaluating if the usability is acceptable.

Chapter References

1. Krug S. (2000), *Don't Make Me Think*, New Riders, Indianapolis.
2. Nielsen J. (1994), "Heuristic Evaluation". In J. Nielsen and R.L. Mack (Eds.), *Usability Inspection Methods*, John Wiley & Sons, New York, pp. 25-62.
3. Muller M.J., Matheson L., Page C., Gallup R. (1998), "Methods & Tools: Participatory Heuristic Evaluation", *Interactions Archive*, Volume 5, Issue 5, Sept./Oct. 13–18.
4. Cato J. (2001), *User-Centred Web Design*, Addison-Wesley, Reading, MA.
5. Jared Spool Interviews:
   http://www.uservision.co.uk/Articles/jaredspool.htm
   (Interview with Jared Spool, *Interfaces Magazine*, British HCI Group, Aug. 2002).
   http://www.usabilitynews.com/news/article432.asp
   (Feature: "Jared Spool, A Man with a Task", May 7, 2002).
6. Badre A. N. (2002), *Shaping Web Usability: Interaction Design in Context*, Addison-Wesley, Reading, MA.
7. Barber W., and Badre A. (1998), "Culturability: The Merging of Culture and Usability", 4th *Conference on Human Factors and the Web, 1998* (http://www.research.microsoft.com/users/marycz/hfweb98/barber).
8. Nielsen J., and Molich R. (1990), "Heuristic Evaluation of User Interfaces", *CHI '90 Proceedings* (April 1990).
9. Perfetti C. (2003), "Usability Testing Best Practices: An Interview with Rolf Molich", http://www.uie.com/articles/molich_interview/.
10. Rubin J. (1994), *Handbook of Usability Testing*, John Wiley & Sons, New York.

CHAPTER FOUR

Aesthetics and Websites

Overview

Aesthetics is concerned with our sensory perceptions and responses to everything and anything we meet and observe around us. In this chapter, we discuss the wider subject of aesthetics and relate aesthetics to the context of websites and website design, concluding with an analysis of some example types of websites. The study of aesthetics dates back to our early beginnings and reaches across almost all disciplines. It is a deep subject and one that cannot be completely addressed in one chapter, or indeed even a dedicated book, but we try to bring several threads of thought together here and in doing so embark on wider research into aesthetics.

Give and Gain

If you give time to this chapter (let's say 45 minutes or so, plus time for the exercises), this is what you will gain:

- an awareness of a background to the topic of aesthetics;
- an introduction to the variety and range of aesthetics that relate to the numerous types of websites;
- the encouragement to be sensitive to aesthetic needs and possibilities for websites and to be creative in attempts to produce appropriate designs.

Introduction to Aesthetics

It is recognised that there are at least four types of 'pleasure' that need to be considered when designing any product [1]:

- Physio-pleasure – pleasure derived from the senses of touch, smell, etc.; for example, the smooth curves of a designer telephone or the smell of a new car.
- Socio-pleasure – pleasure gained from interaction with others and/or the association of 'social identity/gathering'.
- Psycho-pleasure – pleasure from the satisfaction felt when a task is successfully completed, especially if in a pleasurable way. This is closely related to usability.
- Ideo-pleasure – the most abstract pleasure and consisting of the values that an item embodies, such as a concept, or perhaps appealing to conscientious feelings (e.g., environmental protection, freedom, etc.).

According to Immanuel Kant (1724–1804), in aesthetic judgments (i.e., 'judgments of taste'), there are three distinct features that must be present [3]:

(i)   taking pleasure because we judge something to be beautiful (and not a judgment of beauty purely because we find something pleasurable);

(ii)   judgments should be universal (or expected to be universal) and necessary (reactions based on common sense);

(iii)   objects judged to be beautiful appear to be 'purposeful', even though they might not actually have any particular practical purpose.

Aesthetics is widely seen [2] as a very important part of our needs as human beings, as the following diagram illustrates (Fig. 4.1).

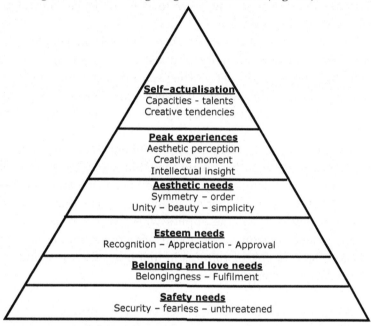

Fig. 4.1: Hierarchy of needs (after Abraham Maslow)

Aesthetic needs are illustrated as being one of our key needs, and aesthetics can be epitomised by 'symmetry, order, and beauty'.

The subject of aesthetics is not new, and in fact many philosophers, from the time of Plato to Aristotle, Hegel, Kant, and many others, have tried to explain and define this complex subject. It commonly concerned nature and works of art such as paintings, sculptures, music, and crafts, for example. In most dictionaries and many philosophy books, 'aesthetics' has been defined as a branch of philosophy that deals with 'beauty' and 'taste'. It comes from the Greek word *aisthétikos* (perception through the senses).

The aesthetic of an item or object is not one special thing, way, or rule that one can apply to or embed in the objects or subjects to end up with an aesthetic value. The human complex sense of appeal in each person can be different from that of others and because of that it is impossible to come up with any specific scientific rule or method for applying aesthetics. However, if aesthetics means perception through the senses, then it will be helpful if we briefly look at our connection, as human beings, of sensory perception to aesthetic awareness.

In the journey of life, we collect information through our five, possibly six, senses. People are in search of objects and subjects that appeal to them from the day they are born. They learn to like and dislike and choose from among the things around them.

Culture, traditions, and society play a big role in people's learning experiences, behaviour, creativity, and tastes in everything; for example, food, clothes, music, and poetry. They can influence one's learning and recognition, evolving through life with new experiences, ways, and ideas to affect a person's perception and judgments of what is pleasing them or not.

We have the ability to imagine, and that helps us to connect different information together to either create something new or recognise things. For example, if we listen to music that we have never heard before, it is the feeling that we get from that music that helps us judge it as a good or bad piece of music. The same applies when we see something, pass a place and smell something, or touch something rough or soft. We understand the meaning of softness in that basically it does not disturb our skin and might even please us.

> "We should not pretend to understand the world only by
> the intellect; we apprehend it just as much by feeling"
> (Carl Jung, [4])

Nature has the most perfect aesthetic in the whole universe. Everything is created in the most amazing way, and the concern for detail is beyond understanding. There are reasons for every detail added to anything and everything. When we look at every object from flowers to humans there are colours and shapes added to distinguish one from another, to attract, protect, or assist survival, and many other reasons. Almost universally, nature produces a feeling of well-being, awe, comfort, and belonging. It is the *aesthetics* of nature that play a big part in creating these impacts.

Websites – The Basics

With the advancement in Web technology and the wide availability of powerful software, it has become easy for almost everyone with IT skills to have a website for the presentation of their interests, products, and/or service available worldwide. When people required beautiful and pleasing websites, the aesthetic value of the sites became important and noticeable.

What is a website? A page, or set of pages, that bring information to our personal computer or interface, wherever we are. They can be just like a few pages of a book or magazine, or they can be like TV websites that contain text, images, videos, sound, and different programs and films that make an environment that everybody, no matter what age, can find of use. Whatever the aim of the website, it needs pages that are visual and most probably interactive.

All successful websites need to be technically strong in such a way that there is compatibility with different browsers and platforms. If we call this the skeleton, then we need to add flesh and in some cases elaborate by giving it appropriate makeup to make it aesthetically pleasing. The skeleton and the flesh, must always work together otherwise the website will not give a good result.

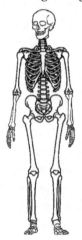

Imagine a human body (Fig. 4.3), that moves by its skeleton (Fig. 4.2). The same number and order of bones in every healthy human being function through the body's inner organs (the same organs usually in every human body) but almost always the body is identified and judged by its 'outer' look; by the 'layout' of items and attributes – such as the colour of eyes, hair, skin, and voice, for example.

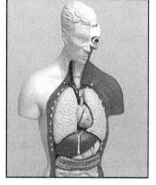

Fig. 4.2: Skeleton

Fig. 4.3: Anatomy [14]
(Humbrol)

These, together with the innermost side – the personality, thoughts, and character – are the important factors that make us individuals and different from others. It is those elements that put flesh on the skeleton. Designers bring life to the pages with shapes, objects, colours, layouts, and ways for interaction and the innermost concept for the site. Therefore, we need to be aware of each component's properties as an individual and in relation to the other items to make the information presented understandable and pleasurable for users.

Beautiful foods always attract people, but what happens if they are not edible for whatever reason? They could be poisonous or not agree with our taste. In this regard we would also like to mention the importance of ethics in relation to aesthetics. There are so many websites that look good and usable but are not accepted by society or some societies because of their content. Therefore, subjectivity and objectivity on the websites are important.

The vast Web environment has the potential to hold any representational elements created outside of that environment such as text, images, animation, video, and sound. Each element by itself can carry some subjective and objective aesthetic value but those one or two items cannot necessarily make the whole website aesthetically strong. The way that all elements are placed on the page can bring harmony to that page. Each element's properties, such as shape, colour, and position, contribute to the harmonious effect on the surface and, if not considered carefully, can give a negative result. We almost always look at the webpage as a whole; therefore the placement of the items in order and harmony and their relationship to each other is something important and worth remembering. Bringing things together into a 'unity of form and content' is suggested as a way to create the right aesthetic [7].

People don't usually open a website to look at the 'beauty' of it – it is something that usually gets noticed when or if something is wrong or is very strong. It is the user's satisfaction resulting from their positive experiences and emotional responses that contributes to the aesthetic value of a website.

Web design is relatively young but has come a long way in its short life. It first started with simple sets of code that created very basic text documents, but it has evolved into a very complex and sophisticated domain that acts as an opportunity for providing or acquiring information, trade, learning, and entertainment. It has created a new global virtual audio-visual culture and because of its speed, interactivity, and ease of accessibility, it has opened up new potentials in any context for almost all kinds of information for people of any age around the world.

The Homepage – The Entrance Door

The homepage is usually the first main page seen and used in a website. It is an important point, as it is like the entrance door to a whole new experience – the point of departure. It suggests the identity of the website and can give an immediate impression for the rest of the content [9]. It is like the entrance door to a shop that invites people to come in and browse and find what they are looking for. Therefore it needs to be inviting and pleasant to bring people in, and this is where the users' journey starts - they first experience by looking and then by interaction. At this stage, users need to look and find their way through to get to what they have come there for in the first place, without *struggling* to find their way.

It can be very effective to employ a 'visual' designer to help with the website design (i.e., not an IT specialist) – especially for the homepage. A website designed by a designer is *pregnant with aesthetics* – like a designer shop window (Figs. 4.4 [see plate 2] and 4.5 [see plate 6]).

Fig. 4.4: http://www.ungaro.com   Fig. 4.5: www.harveynichols.com

If the users are provided with a good and clear navigational route, they should have a pleasant experience throughout that journey. Visible buttons that clearly show the route using iconic symbols or pictures, or with clear text, are often a very helpful approach. Some websites, however, conceptually might aim at a user experience that has more intrigue or mystery, and this would then need to be reflected in the navigation design.

Imagine going to a very large multistory building and trying to see a person, and the names of the people or companies are not on the doorbells. The first question coming to our head is, "Which one is it?" The first reaction probably would be to ring some bells randomly, and after pressing a few wrong bells that would be frustrating and time consuming. One most likely would give up without any success. It is similar to the first experience of the user on a website. However, the users can become familiar with the websites that they regularly have to use, for example, using their bank website to pay the bills, transfer money, see their statement, etc. (Figs. 4.6 and 4.7). Therefore the difficulty is just at the beginning for the unfamiliar users, and those are the main groups that need to be considered.

Fig. 4.6: www.barclay.co.uk   Fig. 4.7: www.hsbc.co.uk

It is the aesthetic qualities together with usability characteristics and the purpose(s) features that define the nature of a website. The intentions have to be matched by reality – i.e., the elements of the site must operate successfully in a pragmatic way (functionality). There is no point in designing a beautiful and unique door handle if it does not fit or work on the door and function as it should to open the door. Creative flair is also important. In a sense, it is creativity that produces the perfect aesthetic.

Badre [5] discusses the importance of aesthetics, and its role in affecting the usability of a website, and proposes that designers need to strike a balance between aesthetics and usability. Attention is drawn to the possibility that the 'art' of a website's design could adversely impact usability [5]. We suggest that it is also (and equally, perhaps) possible for bad usability/functionality to kill the aesthetic value. Aesthetics and usability are interrelated and almost inseparable.

The Layout

The arrangement of items in a coherent manner to help the user find objects or links to the desired information is something we aim for in the layout of a webpage. To design a website that has aesthetic *value*, we need some understanding and familiarity with the traditional principles of design that have guided many successful architects, artists, and designers from different disciplines. The main principles are

- Balance
- Proportion
- Rhythm
- Unity

The aim is to position items on the page in a way that makes the page pleasing and the contents appropriately easy to find by users' interaction. Users always see one complete page at a time, so *dividing* the space is an important factor in arranging the contents (text, headlines, pictures, logos, buttons, etc) that need to go on a page.

There are different ways to fill the page, but one of the ways that has given a positive result in the past for finding the items is to divide the space and information so that items are placed appropriately in relation to each other – giving a 'harmonic' effect by using a 'grid' format.

Clear rules of aesthetic proportion were laid down from very early times. Although many designers prefer to rely on their intuitive sense of proportion when they are designing a page, it is useful to have an understanding of the principles of proportion in determining the correct division of the space within a layout. In the following paragraphs, we will briefly look at the history of proportion and the 'grid' and see how they came about and the importance of using the grid as one of the effective ways in creating aesthetic proportion.

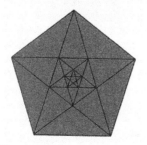

Greek architects Phidias and Ictinus demonstrated the design potential of the division of a line into extreme and mean ratios (see Fig. 4.8), which was the basis for the division of space and was called the 'golden section'.

Fig. 4.8: The golden section

It is based on a pentagon, a regular five-sided polygon that together with its related pentagrams consists of scores of golden sections, but this was not the only guide to aesthetic proportion, as many combinations of simple squares also play a big role in dividing the space.

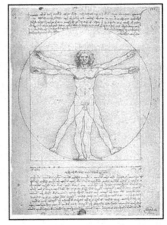

The classic drawing of the Vitruvian Man (Fig. 4.9) establishes the basic symmetry of the square. The famous drawing by Leonardo da Vinci was made around the year 1490 in one of his journals. It depicts a male figure in two superimposed positions with his arms apart and simultaneously inscribed in a circle and square. The drawing and text are sometimes called the 'Canon of Proportions' [11].

Fig. 4.9: The Vitruvian Man

Many years after the Vitruvian Man, Le Corbusier, a well-known architect of the 20th century who was concerned with architectural form, developed a design system based on the golden section and human proportions. He called his system 'The Modulor' (Fig. 4.10) and built it around three main points of anatomy – the top of the head, the solar plexus, and the tip of the raised hand [6].

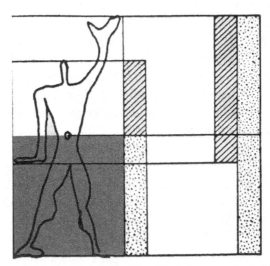

Fig. 4.10: The Modulor

Although Le Corbusier was mainly concerned with architectural form designed using the Modulor, it didn't take very long to notice its potential for other areas, including the design of printed pages. It inspired the typographic designers and was used for the design of printed pages such as newspapers and magazines at the time, and still today similar grid systems have been adopted by new media and website designers.

The grid is made of the vertical and horizontal lines that divide the space before designing a page and help position the contents such as text and images, and when it is used with skill and attention to the contents and their relationship together can result in very effective pages. The aesthetic value in the visual communication in general terms, and especially in the context of web design, not only derives from the words and images but it is the attention and emphasis that is given to their positioning/layout that can make the impact by engaging the user.

In Figs. 4.11 [see plate 11] and 4.12 [see plate 12], we see two examples of popular websites that are used by a large number of users globally and use a grid system for placing and fitting all the information, which also needs to change minute by minute.

Fig. 4.11: BBC homepage   Fig. 4.12: CNN homepage

Although the use of the grid can give a sense of cohesion to the overall design, we should not let it *dominate* our ideas for design. Colour plays a big role in emphasising and delineating webpage layout. It is used in backgrounds, text, and imagery to help divide and represent information. Effects (on images and/or sound) are used to show and create the appropriate atmospheres and impacts.

Type and Typography

Throughout history, letters and type have been used in most languages either on their own or combined with other graphic elements to convey messages or identity.

Fig. 4.13: Sample from www.bemboszoo.com

We are all familiar with different ways of using type either as text for communication (e.g., letters, books, newspapers) or recognising it as signs, logos, messages, etc., but type is also being used creatively in different ways; for example, in calligraphy or making up shapes for many purposes. Roberto de Vicq de Cumptich, the creator of Bembo's zoo [10], created an interactive educational animation where shapes of the animals are creatively made by the movement of letters and are combined with the sound of the animals (Fig. 4.13 [see plate 3]).

'Typeface' is the name given to describe the style of lettering or symbols, and this terminology relates to the tradition of typesetting. In the world of computers, the digital type faces are called fonts, and each font is identified by a special name.

Playing with the size and manipulating the letters can sometimes produce very strong and pleasing effects that can add immediate meaning to the rest of the content (Fig. 4.14 [see plate 7]). Brody [13] states that typography can have levels that are communicated simultaneously with the words. Typography can also draw the attention of the users and add aesthetic value to the page(s). It could play a big role in headings, signs, buttons, or other important factors.

Fig. 4.14: Creative typeface use [12]

Aesthetic Judgment

The Internet is a multicultural medium, and each website carries its own aesthetics in relation to its content to serve its target audience, although it is accessible by the global world.

Sometimes there could be limitations in understanding some websites such as different languages, colours, and symbols with special meanings for a specific purpose. To understand some of those, one needs to understand the related culture to appreciate what is presented. Therefore, the idea of judgment of aesthetics cannot easily be formulated and is more *relative* than *absolute*. Perhaps the aesthetic of the website design is the 'satisfaction' of the users. There are some websites with content that already carries strong aesthetics – such as those with strong creative elements (e.g., fashion). The layout and structural composition/design of the content must *work* with the aesthetics of the content itself. There are many things that can affect the user's experience and hence damage the aesthetic experience:

- Nonfunctional items
- Poor combinations or positioning of items
- Bad navigation
- Wrong size text
- Clogged page
- Use of many or wrong colours
- Pages that would not fit the screen
- Unnecessary sound/music
- Sudden changes to the existing pages of the websites

One of the problems that is evident is the way people design the webpages in the same way as magazines and books and other things that existed for years and with which we all are familiar. But the web design should be different because of its screen nature and its interactivity. We should remember that watching the screen and reading information that could be extremely tiring if, for example, the right fonts and size or colour are not chosen for the design of that page. A congested website filled with lots of information can in fact kill the aesthetic value of it, as it can cause confusion followed by frustration. Unnecessary sound or songs on the page can sometimes destroy or damage the visual aesthetic. Well-chosen sonic material can, however, enhance an aesthetic.

Let's say we have designed a website that is usable and beautiful but not appropriate for the subject – another thing that can annoy the user. Unfortunately, the tools that are introduced by different programs (e.g., templates for ready-made buttons) give a kind of uniformity to many webpages and show lack of imagination and creativity that can bore the viewer. People use them because they are available and ready but possibly do not think of the appropriateness of them for their websites. It is like the character and charisma of a person – the detail, identity, and suitability matters to the impression made.

How can we judge the aesthetics of a website? Is it possible to make something that can have an appealing effect on *every* viewer? This is global communication design we are talking about, not something that is produced for one person. So, to find a way to satisfy all viewers can be impossible. However, the nature of the subject on the website can be a good guide to researching the audience, and that can help us to look at the culture and needs of that audience.

Interactivity

With webpages, we expect the users to look at a certain page and get information about something, somewhere, or somebody, and sometimes our intention is to take them on a journey and let them explore different things. For example, the BBC – for years known to people as the British radio and television domain – first went outside Britain to a few countries by satellite and then became global through its website [8]. The content of the BBC website [8] serves and entertains almost all ages all over the world. As some of the content is the same as what they show on television or broadcast on the radio, there are some people who just use the computer as a radio or television. Clearly the website has to cater for a wide audience, and yet it has distinct styles for its various sections and pages according to what is deemed to be the target audiences for those pages (presumingly matching the audiences for the terrestrial subject matter such as the different BBC radio stations). Perhaps sometimes it is the same people but with different moods/expectations. In contrast, the BBC *homepage* possibly targets 'average' aesthetic expectations and preferences.

In almost all cases, websites engage the users and force them indirectly to interact with the content on the screen to get to the information they need by using elements such as buttons.

This new culture is adapting many things, such as pictures, sounds, shapes, forms, pictograms, and signs – taken from the ordinary everyday culture of the West or East. The most obvious reason for that is the common familiarities that people have developed through using some items, and in this way their perception has been developed over the years. For example, people have become used to the control system on the audio and video systems; they interact with the system using the direction of the arrows for going forward and rewind and symbols for play, pause, and stop. However, those graphics do not look exactly the same on all items – they vary according to the quest to create a design with the right aesthetic (although they do the same *jobs* in most cases).

It is human nature to always search for something new, whether products, places, hobbies, or whatever, no matter how perfect something is, as there is always a time in life for everything. Sometimes there is a need to change or refresh the look of a website to give a new experience. Throughout history, we have witnessed different kinds of changes in products as consequences of new ways of understanding human needs and evolutions in technology and design.

In the past two decades, with the fast evolution in digital technology, the computer (which was once only available to limited groups) has found its way into most people's homes and offices for different uses. The need for interaction has created many research opportunities in various areas (e.g., HCI – human–computer interaction) to tackle usability problems as well as improvements and new ideas for the future. Interacting with computers has steadily become an everyday task. The majority of the people around the world use computers directly or indirectly and have to some extent learned to press the buttons by having learned the look of the icons previously or get to what they want by using the menus. What the Internet has done is brought the systems that we had used before to our screens, where we can listen to music instead of turning on the radio or watching television and can read the latest news instead of waiting for newspapers to print, pay the bills instead of going to the bank, buy the books that we want, and do our daily supermarket shopping. This list can go on and on – a culture that has very quickly become a part of our lives. In the process of this fast jump, it was obvious that tackling the functionality and usability had to become a necessity and priority, but as the multimedia scope grew further at the same time, and with the involvement of many expert designers, it was now time also to be much more aware of the aesthetic issues. We have to be concerned about the look and the user experience of the website – making it a much more appealing experience for the users.

Beginning an Aesthetic Design

When we start designing a Web page, we usually have a blank two-dimensional page that says or shows nothing, and therefore it has no character at this stage. It only starts to form when different kinds of elements are thrown into the blank page(s) to represent the content according to the context for serving the needs of the users. It is those elements that bring life to the pages with their shape, size, colour, meaning, and place. Therefore we need to be aware of each component's properties individually and in relation to the other items to make the information presented appealing by being understandable and pleasurable to use.

The aim of many websites is to be designed in a way intended to provoke the users to engage with the theme of the website. Remember, websites are a form of art, which must be

> "…made for human beings and not for intellectual machines, appealing not only through the formal arrangement but through the subject matter, that is through the content or meaning of such arrangement." [7]

The user is the audience, and classifying them from the beginning will help us to come up with a better result. For example, what is pleasing for the teenage audience does not usually satisfy people in their 40s or 50s. The teenagers do not normally enjoy calm background music on the sites they view. They are usually seeking excitement!

There are times when you as a web designer are not in control of designing some or most of the web contents and your role is to arrange all the elements and information in an aesthetically pleasing way within a given space. For example, one could be given items that have been designed previously and/or a company could have a known and recognised logo and does not want that to be changed in any way, as it is their identity by which people recognise them. Sometimes the colour(s) of the logo might clash with the colours of the other components. Therefore it is important to choose some attributes and perhaps effects of some kind in order to get a positive result at the end.

Visiting some websites for the first time is like going through an adventurous journey, and through this journey the subjective and objective contents can produce a peculiar atmosphere and affect the general mood. Sometimes one can be put in a new frame of mind for serious information, comedy, or tragic news and experience different feelings such as joy, happiness, sadness, satisfaction, dissatisfaction, disgust, etc. One good example is the BBC website [8], which provides information and entertainment to satisfy the needs and desires of almost any age group; for example, cartoons and games for very young children, learning zones and pop music for teenagers, and serious and comedy programmes and political reviews for adults. The design of the website has to take into account these varying aesthetic needs.

The aesthetic of any website is defined by the *aesthetic experience*, which in turn we propose has the following ingredients:

- how easy it is to find the information or item required;
- the extent to which the content found satisfies the desires;
- the way of presenting the information/items;
- mood/characteristics of the person;
- mode of use (of the website by the user);
- expectations of the person;
- the surrounding environment whilst experiencing the website.

Hence, the aesthetic experience can be different for different people and for the same people on different occasions.

Website Review

In Chapter 3, we presented a categorisation of websites as a development of earlier work by Badre [5]. In this section, we analyse a selection, of these website types from the perspective of aesthetics (please refer to Tables 4.1–4.3) by showing a range of example types of websites and indicating the notions of 'attention' and the 'appeal, aesthetic, and emotional' experiences typical for those types.

Table 4.1: Entertainment type websites

Entertainment e.g. www.bbc.co.uk	Type of Service	Attention	Appeal, Aesthetic and Emotional Experience
Television	Politics Reviews Live and latest news, audio and video in different languages List of programmes Archived programmes	Watching Listening Sending comments	Awareness, joy, sadness, happiness, convenience, satisfaction
Edutainment	Multimedia Learning by listening and watching Interactive test Educational and interactive games (children/adult)	Learning by listening, watching and interaction	Motivation, fun, joy, excitement, satisfaction
Art	Movies Theatre Exhibitions Music Installations Photography	Listening Watching Learning Experience	Fun, fear, joy, excitement, calmness, meditative, reflective

Table 4.2: General interest type websites

Information Websites e.g. www.expedia.com	Type of Service	Attention	Appeal/ Aesthetic and Emotional Experience

Travel	Information
	Location
	Map
	Attractions
	Climate
	Travel news
	Booking/buying
	   tickets
	Accommodation
	   information
		Finding
		Awareness
		Contact
		Viewing
		Reading
		Planning
		Experience
			Satisfaction
			Appreciation
			Happiness
			Excitement
			Anticipation

Property	View/choose Contact Rent/buy Sell Guidance	Finding Viewing Reading Dreaming	Excitement Satisfaction Intrigue

Table 4.3: Miscellaneous type websites

	Type of Service	Attention	Appeal/ Aesthetic and Emotional Experience
Fun website: Interactive games, casino, gambling e.g. www.spinpalace.com www.casinoonnet.com	Providing choices Security Payment options Fun Role-play	Watching Making choices Playing/gambling Immersive	Excitement Surprise Confidence Fun, joy, magnetism Disappointment
Promotion/retail website: Fashion design e.g. www.giorgioarmani.com www.chanel.com http://www.nordstrom.com	Presentation Information Awareness Suggestions Sale Provision Lifestyle	Watching Listening New ideas/trends Making choices Contact Buy	Inspiration Motivation Joy, fun Desire, envy Excitement Convenience Satisfaction
Community website: e.g. http://www.persian911.com	Presentation (pictures, music, movies) News (political, cultural) Information Awareness Suggestions Contacts Support	Watching Listening Contact Participation Contribution	Community Togetherness Nostalgia Inspiration, motivation Joy, fun Desire, envy Excitement Frustration Convenience

Chapter Exercises

Seminar Topics

1. Debate the extent to which you feel usability design could be regarded as being the same as aesthetics design?
2. "Users cannot evaluate aesthetics – a specialist is needed." Discuss this statement.
3. Compare and contrast the aesthetics of an effective solicitor's website and that of a website for hip-hop or for jazz music or for some other style of music.

Tutorial Exercises

1. Name at least two types of pleasure that should be considered when designing for aesthetics.
2. What is the conceptual basis for the layout of typical news media website pages?
3. State at least two aesthetic characteristics likely to be experienced with an entertainment website and a community type website.

Case Study

1. Jot down what you regard as being the main aesthetic characteristics that might best be associated with your project website.
2. Surf the Web to look at websites within and outside the genre of your project website. Analyse the aesthetics and the design ideas adopted to create those experiences.
3. Write down as many creative ideas as possible – to target the desired aesthetics for your website – that you might try when prototyping your website later.

Chapter References

1. Jordan P. W. and Green W. S. (Eds.) (2001), *Pleasure with Products: Beyond Usability,* Taylor & Francis, London.
2. Maslow A. (1998), *Toward a Psychology of Being,* 3rd edition, John Wiley & Sons, New York.
3. Kant I. (1987), *Critique of Judgment*, Trans. Werner Pluhar, Hackett Publishing Company, Indianapolis.
4. Jung, C. http://en.wikiquote.org/wiki/Carl_Jung.
5. Badre A. N. (2002), *Shaping Web Usability: Interaction Design in in Context* (http://www.research.microsoft.com/users/marycz/ hfweb98/barber).
6. Hurlburt A. (1979), *The Grid*, Barrie & Jenkins Ltd.
7. Langfield H. S. (1920), *Aesthetic Attitude*, Harcourt, Brace and Howe
8. www.bbc.co.uk.
9. Krug S. (2000), *Don't Make Me Think*, New Riders, Indianapolis
10. www.bemboszoo.com.
11. www.localcolorart.com.
12. http://www.researchstudios.com/home/006-neville-brody/ NEVILLE_home.php.
13. http://www.apple.com/pro/design/brody/index3.html.
14. http://news.bbc.co.uk/1/hi/uk/754680.stm.

Section 2: Methodology Process

CHAPTER FIVE

Requirements – Initial Acquisition

Overview

This chapter is where the practical work begins and deals with the details of the first stages of a website design methodology (analysis and requirements specification). There are three steps involved in this chapter – with tutorial/seminar and case study exercises at the end of each step – designed to reinforce understanding of the recommended methodology and to help you progressively work on your own chosen case study project.

The overall process of a methodology for website design/implementation is described and explained, and each step is covered in detail. All of the documentation needed to complete a website design project using the methodology is presented and explained, with a 'worked' example presented to illustrate how to utilise documentation as part of a design process.

Please note that in advance of beginning work as described in this chapter, there is some preparation needed ahead of the project. This is general preparation and essentially involves building up people and other resources to be ready to tackle the range of website design tasks that are to be faced. This aspect was discussed in Chapter 2 and, in summary, it is necessary to have access to sufficient skills in analysis, design, programming (at HTML and generator software levels), graphics, multimedia capture and design, layout/structure design and evaluation, and (in the case of a team project) team leading, informal/formal communication, and project management.

Before commencing a project, a program of personnel recruitment and training may be needed, depending on the size of the project and the previous experience of an individual and/or team. Some projects are completed by a small team (perhaps one person only), and in this case the person needs to combine a mixture of the required skills and roles in the project. Awareness of and familiarity with the adopted methodology is also needed. Software and hardware necessary for project completion need to be set in place. Due to the lead times associated with delivery, installation, and training, this aspect needs to be planned and initiated well in advance.

Give and Gain

If you give time to this chapter (let's say 50 minutes or so, plus time for the exercises), this is what you will gain:

- an understanding about the first three steps of a website design project (project startup, time and task analysis, and initial requirements gathering) – what needs to be done, why, and how;
- knowledge and practical experience of following through these first three steps and using the design documentation as part of the process.

5.1 Step 1: Project Startup

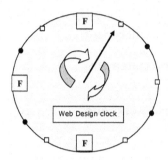

This is the initial step for the website design project. It is where we establish the scope, constraints and gaps, main ambitions, ground rules, cost budgets, team formation, and role-player structure for the project.

The information needed for this step may (partly) have already been ascertained, but almost certainly there will be the need for clarifying, verifying, and completing acquisition. Interviews, questionnaires, and informal discussions are all useful methods to employ.

Typically this initial information gathering and project planning will be carried out by one or two key project personnel who often will be the people who design and implement the website (if a small team project) or become lead analysts and/or project managers for the project. The active involvement of the user-clients is important here, as in all stages of a project. The aspects that need to be discussed and detailed are as follows and fall into two broad groups (Fig. 5.1).

Developer/User-Client Responsibilities	Developer Responsibilities
• website scope • perceived constraints and gaps in resources • main ambitions • project ground rules • available/required budgets • preferred project role structuring • user-client rep selection • timescales	• detailed development budgeting • development team formation and role selection, • milestones

Fig. 5.1: Project startup information

Possibly the very first piece of design documentation to complete is the website scenario (Table 5.1), which provides a summary of the intentions for the website and the main known characteristics of the audience targeted. This provides a concise initial view of the scope, depth, and purpose(s) of the website to be designed and developed. The audience characteristics should include some mention of expectations and likely design preferences, where possible. A title is given to the website, which at this stage might be a working title. Once the title is agreed, the focus will become clear and the whole design process will benefit.

Table 5.1: Website scenario statement

Website Title	"World Religions"
Summary of website intentions	To generate awareness and an educational resource on the topic of the 'main' religions followed around the world.
Targeted audience characteristics	Targeted mainly at the younger age range (school ages) but hopefully also of interest to adults. Readers are likely to be unfamiliar with some of the religions. Attractiveness, clarity, accuracy, and accessibility (language/format) are important.
Website Scenario Statement **Website ID (name):** **Author (of this form):** **Date:**	World Religions FK Week 1

For easy reference later, a 'short name' can be given to identify the website, and the name of the developer/designer creating the form is stated, along with the date. Typical entries to this documentation are shown in Table 5.1, which describes a real website project (based on level 2 student project work) used as a simple case study throughout this book.

Table 5.2: Project attributes

Attribute	Detail
Website title	**"World Religions"**
Scope	Small/medium/high profile
General description	Provide a general resource for teenagers/young adults researching a wide range of popular religions
Constraints and gaps	**Technology?:** Possibly some restrictions regarding streaming (webserver facilities needed) **Skills?:** Ned to further develop skills in DHTML and web multimedia **Financial?:** МА **Action/comments?** • Check available facilities/rights on webserver • Study skills workshops
Main aims and ambitions	1. website to be a 'one-stop' area whereby mainly older children and adults alike can find a clear overview of prominent religions of the world 2. extensive amount of clarity and accuracy 3. target young/varied age audience
Team formation/ role-play structure	**Particular issues?** МА (individual project) **Structure detail?**
Ground rules	**Responsibility/authorities:** МА (individual project) **Communications/reporting:** **Other (e.g., meeting frequency, user/client involvement, technical)** File naming – use 'nameVx' convention
Cost budgets/ timescale	Cost amounts, approval?: МА Deadline for completion?: Week 10
Project Attributes Report **Website ID (name):** **Date:**	World Religions Week 1

Once the startup information about the project has all been gathered and agreed, it should be possible to complete the forms shown in Table 5.1 and Table 5.2. The website scenario statement crystallises the gathered requirements into simple descriptions of two aspects – a summary of website intentions (i.e., the main ambitions regarding the impact and consequences of the website) and target audience characteristics (forming an awareness of who the site is targeted at and their expectations/needs). Importantly, a title is also given to the website project.

Table 5.2 requires more detail and a wider range of information. If any of the aspects seem incomplete or inconclusive, then more information gathering and information analysis needs to take place.

Where there is a large section of text (and/or diagrams) needed for a particular item, this should be detailed on a separate piece of paper – with brief summary information only in the table itself. Small increases in space available can be easily created by using electronic copies of the forms.

The website title is taken from the website scenario form, completed earlier, and is used on all subsequent documentation as a quick ID of the project (a team might be busy on more than one project, and so this labeling can be very useful). The scope of the project entails the consideration of the depth and breadth that the website is intended to cover. Is it a small site to establish a minimum web presence, is it a high-profile site to be used as a flagship for a large corporation, or something in between? The appropriate classification of 'small, medium, or large' is highlighted.

A general description of the website is useful here and will be expanded and made more specific in the next step (by identifying website genre and subtype definitions). The general description is a crystallised and refined version of the content of Table 5.1. This may strike you as being a little repetitious, but this kind of consolidation and clarification helps with reinforcing, evolving, and firmly establishing the intentions for the site.

Are there technology, skills, or financial constraints and/or gaps? To what extent do these constraints impinge on the overall intentions and hopes for the site? Are there any gaps that need to be resolved before or during the project and, if so, what action can be taken?

It is very important to identify and understand the main aims and ambitions of the site at this early stage in the life cycle of the website. Misunderstandings and lack of clarity or comprehensiveness can be very punishing later – they must be 'ironed out' and resolved in this first step.

Small problematic issues can so easily become very troublesome burdens later in the project if ignored or missed at this stage. Aims and ambitions are often surprisingly difficult to extract and define; many people or organisations know they need a website but can find it a major task to elucidate precisely why it is needed and exactly what are the hopes and intended purposes for the site. Work with the users/clients to comprehensively ascertain the key aims and ambitions for the site. The table example given (Table 5.2) shows three items, but there could be more or fewer items stated, depending on the nature of the site.

Your project might not be a team project, but if it is, then effective team formation is crucial, as is role-play structure definition. The project and/or budget size might be such that all of the work is to be carried out by one person (rather than a team). This simplifies matters in some ways but means that the same person has to take on multiple roles. In the table, record any issues that require attention or need to be particularly noted by the project team. A separate sheet should be used to show the hierarchy of the project team and the allocation of roles. The developer team and the wider project team (which includes user/client representatives) need to be formed with care. A complete range of skills, interests, and knowledge has to be present in the teams as a whole, with an overall set of characteristics that match the scope and nature of the project. The members also need to work together in a productive and effective manner, so the mix of personalities has a fundamental impact on productivity and the quality of outcomes.

Closely associated with the selection of team members is the task of deciding and specifying the role-playing structure of the project. Each team member must be clear about their own responsibilities and expectations and the structure of management, control, and authority. The use of design documentation must be stressed as a consistent feature of the project – and its purpose as a design/implementation enabling device, as well as a potential input to future projects, should be emphasised.

The specific team structure will depend on the project and the organisation but will usually include the following roles:

- Project leader
- Project manager
- User and/or client team leader(s)
- User/client representatives

- Developer team
  - o Analysts
  - o Designers
  - o Coders
  - o Content material acquisition
  - o Multimedia editors
  - o Testers
  - o Documenters
  - o Technical support
  - o Group leaders
- Technical support
- Administrative support

For medium or large projects, a list of names and contact details for the various team roles should be constructed and distributed around the team.

What are the ground rules for the project? What are the lines of communication between team members, and how often are there to be meetings and updates across the team? How is the project work to be distributed and managed? To what extent will the users/clients be involved in the process, and what is expected of them? Technical ground rules are also needed – e.g., what method of version control (of files and data) is to be adopted? The main rules should be summarised on the forms, with details expanded on separate sheets if necessary.

Cost budgets are a necessary aspect of any project. A thorough analysis and recognition of what is needed for successful completion early in the project cycle helps with securing that timely budget approval and hence paving the way for an ideal implementation. Overall budget approval is usually needed in advance of project commencement. Budgets need to cover the following costs:

- User/client project time (meetings, design evaluation, etc.)
- Developer team (time/recruitment)
- Software, hardware, and consumables
- Training
- Maintenance and system evolution
- Project management and control

Detailed planning of project tasks, timings, and allocation of team members to the tasks will take place soon in the BWD cycle, together with identifying milestones for the project. At this point, the overall deadline for project completion needs to be established – i.e., a timescale for the project is needed. In the next step of the project process, a detailed task/time analysis will take place (Step 2 of BWD).

Once you are happy that the form is complete and 'tells the story' of what this project is all about, make a final check with the client(s) to make sure that your understandings match.

Exercises

Seminar Topics

1. Does every website design project need the *same* ground rules? Discuss influences and needs.
2. Discuss what you would expect to be the potential conflicts and 'grey areas' with regard to project roles and role structures?
3. Estimates of cost and timescale figures can prove to be inaccurate. Discuss any impacts on a project.

Tutorial Exercises

1. Name one project aspect each that is the responsibility of developers, of users/clients, and is a shared responsibility.
2. List the eight *project attributes* that need to be identified and described in BWD Step 1?
3. Give two examples of 'ground rules' that need establishing at the start of the project.

Case Study

1. Complete the website scenario statement, and the project attributes table for *your* website design project.
2. Make a note of any decision or detail that is difficult to provide accurately at this stage for later follow-up.
3. To what extent are any of the main ambitions for your website at risk of not being achieved? Consider the criticality.

5.2 Step 2: Time and Task Analysis

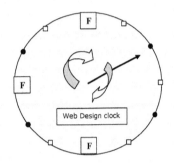

Using the 'project attributes' (Table 5.2) as a starting point, it is possible to determine the detailed task descriptions, estimated time durations, and scheduling. This can be quite a complex task but is very necessary in order for the project to be managed and controlled. It takes time and energy to do this job properly and minimise the risk of any inaccurate estimates or incomplete task lists. Any discrepancies will become apparent eventually and possibly could lead to significant problems later in the project. Hence, revisits to the estimates and task sequence planning need to be made quite frequently so that eventualities and new data can be taken into account. The analysis helps you to plan resources and decide on measures to keep the project on track. Special project management packages are available, and this software can give valuable help with time and task analysis advantages – notably in that updating plans is much easier and quicker. Also, charts and tables can be printed easily for distribution and study around the team. Two disadvantages are that these packages have a learning curve and that the notation style might not match your usual in-house style.

The main activities in this step of the process are:

- Study the project attributes table (already completed in Step 1).
- List the complete set of tasks for the project (i.e., those needed to provide the target deliverables) – hint: the list on p. 31 is a starting point.
- Estimate the resources and time needed for each task.
- Assess risks and plan and apply contingencies for actual or potential problems.
- Schedule tasks after taking into account task dependencies, practical considerations, planned contingencies, and available personnel.

On an ongoing basis, it is necessary to monitor progress and evaluate the project plan and document and refresh the project schedule plan.

At a minimum, visualise the planning using a Gantt chart format (Fig. 5.2). Network analysis is a possible additional approach, useful for identifying the 'critical path' of activities in the project. For each of these project management documentation techniques, it is necessary to establish the following details about the project tasks: durations, dependencies, and resources. Dividing a project into a set of manageable tasks so that dependencies between tasks can be accommodated by the planning is crucial. The alternative is to bury one's head in the sand and hope everything comes together on time and completely – which is too much of a risk to take, bearing in mind the costs of an ineffective, incomplete, or late implementation.

An example of an overview Gantt chart for a typical website project is shown in Fig. 5.2. For a more comprehensive view of how detailed tasks interrelate, a chart is normally drawn where the design/implementation task areas are broken down into component tasks, showing detailed dependencies and sequences of tasks.

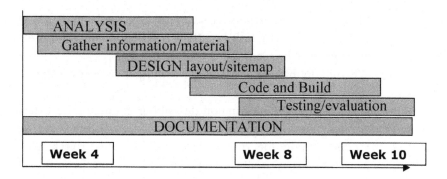

Fig. 5.2: Gantt chart

The chart is drawn to show the lengths (durations) of each task bar and the sequence of when they occur in the project. Each task is drawn in such a position as to illustrate if a task is dependent on another task (i.e., that a task cannot be started until another is completed). When all tasks are included, we see the pattern of tasks beginning and ending and some running parallel. At the point in the chart where the last task ends, we can see the total estimated duration time of the project.

As the project continues, 'actual' times can be added to the chart, and if any tasks overrun (or get completed more quickly), the chart will need updating. Decisions might need to be made on contingencies as well as on rescheduling of tasks/personnel.

The Gantt charts can be made more easily readable by the careful use of colours and labeling. For complex projects, it is useful to have a summary chart plus one or more detailed charts, where the detailed chart shows the summary tasks broken down into finer detail. There are some additional points to note when carrying out an analysis of project tasks and their scheduling:

- Individuals in a project team could concentrate on one task at a time or 'multitask' (depending on experience, task types, project needs/constraints), and this will of course affect the scheduling and total project time.
- Dependencies between tasks are not always immediately apparent, but if any are missed this can have quite an adverse effect on scheduling accuracy. Sometimes dependencies are overlooked due to the tasks not being broken down into a sufficient level of detail.
- Identifying a comprehensive set of tasks, recognising dependencies, and estimating task durations is difficult and will improve as experience increases.
- When in doubt, add a reasonable contingency to any estimate.

Milestone charts contain information describing the details and status of the milestones identified for the project. The milestones are key (significant) points along the route to completing the project. These milestones help to break up what might be very large projects, so that the project becomes a sequence of more easily manageable 'phases'. Several phases of a project are much easier to plan and manage than a very large monolithic project, and the presence of identified milestone points means that progress can be monitored at a 'macro' level. Milestones themselves must be identifiable 'completion points' – i.e., it must be clearly obvious whether the milestone has been completed or not (e.g., 'detailed design signed as agreed by team leaders' is a good milestone, and 'understand requirements' is not quite specific enough, as it must be readily possible to recognise that it has been achieved/completed).

Table 5.3 shows an example milestone chart from our example case study. The exact number of milestones depends on the size and nature of the project but should be enough to keep control of the project's progress.

Table 5.3: Milestone chart

ID	Milestone Description	Est. Date	Actual Date	Action / Comments	(Next) Review Date
1	Specify main tasks and draw overall Gantt chart	Week 2	Week 2.5	Less time now for gathering content	Week 6
2	All content material formed (text/images)	Week 6			Week 6
3	Ready for full testing	Week 8			Week 8
4	Complete and document testing	Week 10			Week 10
Milestone Chart **Website Project:** **Date:**			World Religions Weeks 2/3		

For a typical medium-sized website design project, there would be 4–6 milestones, with more for large projects and fewer for small projects. Regular review meetings should include checks of the status of each individual task and also the milestones, possible problems with deadline dates, and actions decided to deal with any problems. The milestone chart acts as a very useful checklist and a thermometer for any impacts made on project progress, the details of which will be revealed more fully via the Gantt chart and/or a network analysis chart. Network analysis uses a simple graphic and arithmetic technique to calculate a total project time based on quite precise but simple modeling of task times, sequences, and dependencies. The consequences of not achieving milestone deadlines can only be realised by also reviewing Gantt and/or critical path analysis charts (in the light of the impact and the end time(s) for tasks that have overrun). They are, however, easy to prepare and understand, and they present crucial information in easy-to-understand summary form.

Exercises

Seminar Topics

1. How would you decide on whether tasks are *really* dependent on another task? Can dependencies between tasks be changed by changing the project in some way?
2. Some believe that Gantt charting and network analysis waste important time. Do you agree? Discuss.
3. Who should do the time and task analyses? Specialists, team members, or team leaders? Why?

Tutorial Exercises

1. What exactly is meant by the term 'milestone'?
2. Explain how Gantt charts are built up and the total project time calculated.
3. What might be the consequence (in project and project charting terms) of a task overrunning?

Case Study

1. Make a list of detailed tasks required to complete *your* website project, and identify any dependencies between tasks.
2. Draw a Gantt chart to illustrate the tasks and your first draft at sequencing the tasks. If a team, make some decisions about who will be completing which task. A critical path analysis could also be made.
3. Identify three or more milestones for your project, and begin the completion of the milestone table.
4. Please remember to revisit the Gantt chart and the milestone chart as your project progresses to review them for any changes and the need for any reaction to the actual task times that transpire.

5.3 Step 3: Initial Requirements Gathering

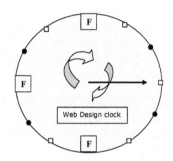

As we commence this third step of the design process, a view has already been formed of the project as a whole and of the main features, needs, and constraints relating to the project website. The project has also been broken down into tasks with estimated durations and sequenced to give a total project time. This step is 'initial require-ments gathering', where the details of the requirements are ascertained and collated; ready for further treatment in the subsequent steps.

In the later steps 4 and 5, the detailed requirements information is translated and crystallised to specify all of the purpose, usability, and aesthetic design needs and the design decisions to match those needs. In the current step, we have the task of establishing the general list of requirements that will form the foundation for considering the details.

Depending on the size of your project, there may now already be a project team in place comprising key role-players. Alternatively, the website might be designed and implemented by only one or two people. If the project is a team project, the task of requirements gathering could be distributed amongst the whole project team as shown in Fig. 5.3. The tasks shown in Fig. 5.3 are iterative – the gathering, documentation, and analysis process will usually need to be repeated a few times until everyone is reasonably satisfied with its completeness and accuracy. A return to 'requirements gathering' might be needed later in the project – for example, for clarifications needed to help with detailed design in later process steps.

Where a project is not a team project (e.g., an individual designing and implementing), there is a need to take on multiple roles during the project – but the core list of tasks remains consistent. It is good practice to document progress and decisions made at each stage within this step, including dates/times, the contributing team members at meetings, and participants in interviews/surveys.

Website Project Role	Tasks
Project leader	Overall management of the requirements gathering process – planning coordination, overall decision making
Project manager	Monitoring, support, and management of the various role-players and the process
User and/or client team leader(s), Analysts	Selecting key personnel to take part in interviews and questionnaire surveys, composing scope and structure of questions and aspects to investigate
Analysts, designers	Detailed design of questionnaires and interview questions and leading interviews/surveys
Analysts, group leaders, designers, User/client representatives	Participation in one-to-one interviews, questionnaire completion, and group discussion sessions. Specification (documented) of requirements from the information gathered
Analysts, user/client representatives, designers, coders, content material acquisition personnel, multimedia editors, testers, documenters , technical support, administrative support	Discussion and the creation of the various items of requirements specification documentation plus feedback/reviews

Fig. 5.3: Project team task distribution (requirements gathering)

The documentation in this step is designed to help gather and record the subject matter and requirements information in a structured and useful way. Each item of documentation feeds into one or more subsequent parts of the design and development process, contributing to the overall and detailed analysis and design. Table 5.4 is an example extract of how an interview/questionnaire can be documented (based on our case study). The questions are formulated so that they collectively will provide information that contributes to enabling the website to be accurately and effectively designed. Information is needed on design preferences/ideas, the required scope of processing, and material to be shown on the site (the 'context'), for example. The nature of the questions will partly depend on who is the interviewee and what becomes a priority for the project. Interviews generally give richer and more comprehensive information, but the use of a questionnaire approach might be the only option in some situations.

The number of questions per project area will vary, as will the number of project areas, and the questions themselves will be different for each project – some will be there to confirm existing knowledge, others to ascertain new facts and information. Depending on the nature of the project, it might be difficult to split the project into separate project areas, in which case make a single list of questions for the whole project. The response sections may need multiple-choice options if that is appropriate for particular questions, and some might need space for diagrams/sketches (and/or large drawings placed on separate sheets). Initial sessions might prompt follow-up sessions to further clarify and expand on information about the content material and the design needs.

The questions utilised are chosen and constructed according to the nature of the website project in hand, and the following are some more examples of questions – ones that would be relevant to most projects.

- Is the site intended for retail, information, entertainment, or a mixture of these, or some other main purpose(s)?
- What key features and style would you like to see in the website?
- Will the website need to be linked to a database, and if so what technical constraints/needs are there?
- What impressions and moods would be ideal to achieve?
- Who is or are the intended audience(s)?
- What do you know about the characteristics/needs of the targeted audience?

Table 5.4: Analysis questionnaire/interview report

Analysis Questionnaire / Interview Report (Roman Catholic Example) Project Area : Website ID:		Christianity Concept World Religions
Question		**Response**
1 What is at the centre of your religion?		Belief in the Trinity – The Father (God), the Son (Jesus), and the Holy Spirit and the Holy Bible
2 Please list special days in your religious calendar.		Good Friday (crucifixion of Jesus) Easter Sunday (resurrection of Jesus) Christmas (Birth of Jesus)
3 Are there any weekly activities normally followed?		Confession (of sins, to priest) Attendance at Sunday Mass service (incl. taking 'communion')
Project area :	Design (general)	
1. What are the main things that the website should provide or allow the user to do?		1. The site should give readily understandable information about the main religions across the world, 2. help with indicating sources of further info, and 3. give independent factual views – enlightening and not being opinionated/dogmatic.
2. Are there any particular preferences regarding usability characteristics?		Locations of information elements (and ways to access them) should be simple and consistent for each religion Visual clues/icons, etc., to be used
3. How do you envisage the aesthetics for the site?		Bright, friendly (approachable), calm/factual, use of symmetry/simple patterns for layout, consistent treatment for all religions covered
Participants:		representatives of R.C. faith, plus analyst
Date/Time/Place:		Week 2/campus

Interviews and questionnaire surveys may need to be carried out several times, and with different people, so that you gain as much information and knowledge about the needs of your project as possible to be able to design the website effectively and appropriately. The more that is gained and understood at this stage, the more effective will be the eventual outcomes. The 'acid test' is whether the information collected will later enable the team to compile a thorough and complete definition of aesthetic, usability, and purpose needs for the website (the completion of these major aspects of a project is covered in the next steps of the process).

Group meetings will need to be held to review and discuss the various findings from the questionnaires and interviews. In every project there will be ambiguities and gaps in knowledge that will need to be resolved arising from the initial requirements gathering process. Group meetings are an effective way of recognising any anomalies, making choices/ decisions, and generating ideas for resolution.

Table 5.5: Analysis meetings report

Issue Discussed	Issue ID	Action/Decision/ Recommendations
Principles/aims (of a religion)	1	Recognised danger of info gained not being entirely representative/complete – need to have multiple sources and compare responses
Audio/video – varying preferences re: content	2	Consider adding more, and/or changing, content on a cyclic basis (e.g., to follow calendar progression)
Analysis Meeting Report **Participants of meeting:** **Date/Time/Place:**		FK Week 3/campus

The example documentation shown in Table 5.5 demonstratess how the output from these meetings can be documented for feeding into the next phases of the design process. Any significant issues discussed and actions, decisions, or recommendations are noted in the table. The issue

ID (Table 5.5) is there to help with cross-referencing between documentations, which helps with subsequent discussions and reviews.

In Chapter 2, several items of design documentation are used to illustrate the general scope and fundamental characteristics of the website genre, the development environment, and the target audience. This documentation helps us see the context of the information gleaned in the requirements analysis interviews. Analyse, and debate within the project team, the particular type of website and specifics of the targeted audience, so that you can select from the given parameters in this documentation to match your website situation. Use highlighter pen(s) to indicate your selections. This set of documentation will be useful input to the next steps of the BWD process specifying detailed design needs for your website.

The final output of this step is a list of the main design requirements identified for the web design project. A simple general list is the intention here, with further processing of the information in the following BWD steps, where the list is expanded into detail and applied to defining detailed requirements and design ideas.

A suggested layout for the requirements list is shown in Table 5.6, and example requirements are shown from our case study. The number of requirements will depend on the project, but typically twenty or more separate identified requirements of the website might be indicated.

The language and general style of expression within the various tables and forms for this stage of the process need to be carefully chosen, so that all team members are familiar with the terms. Effective communication between team members is critically important to the success of the project – especially in these early stages of analysis and design. Misconceptions, misunderstandings, and misrepresentations at this stage can ruin a project and make it very difficult to recover the lost ground later.

Table 5.6: Website design requirements list

ID	Priority Level (1-5) 1=highest	Requirement Description
1	1	Text definition of each religion (main points)
2	2	Visual identification/style for each religion
3	2	Audio examples of worship/creeds/ activities
4	4	Video examples where possible
5	1	Clear explanations of main detailed descriptions
6	1	Consistent navigation (visual style where possible)
7	1	Menu system visible on each page
8	2	Moderate animation/'flashing lights'
9	1/2	Subtle colouring (text/background)
10	2/3	Plenty of images/photos
11	3	Low spec/high spec alternatives
12	1/2	Language use – simple but sincere
13	2	At least 5/6 religions (select main followed)
14	1	Nonjudgmental or 'critical', unbiased
15	1	Thorough, complete, and accurate
16		
17		
18		
19		

Website Design Requirements List	
Website ID (name):	World Religions
Date:	Weeks 2/3

Exercises

Seminar Topics

1. Discuss ways that a project can ensure a user-centred approach.
2. Priorities for items in the website design requirements list (see Table 5.6 are needed. Discuss how these can be determined.
3. Discuss which key questionnaire/interview questions could be added to the examples given in this chapter.

Tutorial Exercises

1. Make a list of the roles in a typical website design project team.
2. What is the 'acid test' for evaluating effectiveness of the information gathered in this step?
3. Table 5.6 shows a template for documenting analysis meetings' results. Why does it have a column for 'issue D'?

Case Study

1. Allocate roles and people to the tasks of questionnaire/interview design and completion in the initial requirements gathering if a team project.
2. Design suitable questions for your questionnaires and/or interviews, and as soon as possible conduct the survey(s) and group meetings and further complete the documentation.
3. Build up, using as a basis information gleaned so far in the project, a web design requirements list for your website.

CHAPTER SIX

Design Needs – Building the Picture

Overview

This chapter describes how we can build on the foundation established via the previous initial steps of the design process and work on the detail of defining purpose, usability, and aesthetic requirements and associated design ideas. These three aspects represent the cornerstone of any website project. The aim is to define in detail their needs and a series of specific design ideas to meet each of those needs.

The chapter concludes with the first of the Review and Reflect steps, where there is a look at the information analysed and the design work completed to confirm whether everything is satisfactory or if further work is needed before progressing to the next phase of the project.

Each of the three steps in this chapter is concluded with seminar, tutorial, and case study exercises designed to help reinforce and increase understanding of BWD and to help you make practical progress with your own case study project. This chapter includes examples of design documentation taken from student project work that forms a case study that we use throughout Chapters 5–8. The examples are intended to illustrate the practicalities of using the documentation and not necessarily a reference set of good or optimum practices. They indicate some typical ideas for design, show how needs can be associated with design, and provide many talking points relating to website design approaches and difficulties.

Give and Gain

If you give time to this chapter (let's say 60 minutes or so, plus the exercises), this is what you will gain:

- an understanding about analysing and defining the purpose, usability, and aesthetic needs of a website, and the assignment of specific associated design ideas;
- knowledge and practical experience of using documentation as part of design work.

6.1 Step 4: Purpose Aspirations Recognition

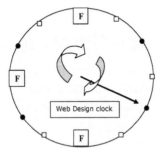

The deliverable of this step could be regarded as the keystone of the whole website development project, as without a clear purpose nothing else can satisfactorily fit into place. Knowledge about the purpose aspirations of a website is not sufficient on its own, however, as appropriate usability and aesthetics are also crucial. These aspects are addressed later in this chapter. In general terms, the overall aims and ambitions of the website have been stated already in previous steps of the project; now, though, we specify them in much more detail and more precisely.

The purpose aspirations table is the first of three critical pieces of documentation. In Step 5 of BWD, it will be the turn of the usability and aesthetic tables. It is in these three tables that we clearly identify the detailed needs for the website design and the intentions that we have for designing to meet each of those needs – i.e., the design ideas.

Imagine you are packing your cases for an overseas holiday, and then compare that task to embarking on this step of your website design project. When packing the cases, you are paving the way for what you wish to do on your holiday – to make sure that you have the things that you need to take full advantage of that holiday time – avoiding the need to waste time and money buying those needed items when you are there and run the risk of the holiday being spoiled. For your website, you can now get your purpose aspirations and interests clear in advance and think of how you can make that all happen with carefully chosen design ideas and pack all of that information into neat and well-organised tables. If a close association can be developed between requirements of these aspects and the actual design, then the project is well on the way to a strong and effective website implementation.

In any system that deals with information, it is crucial to achieve close links between its design (conceptual and detail) and its essential purpose(s). Great designs, but ones that miss the real point of the website's existence, are expensive 'toys'. Great designs that support and enable meaningful and relevant website outcomes are productive investments. The identified purpose aspirations become the focal point for deciding on content, style, characteristics, and presentation. An incomplete and/or unclear purpose will almost certainly lead to an ineffectual and disappointing website – hence careful attention and consideration is needed. Let's look at Table 6.1 (Purpose aspirations table).

It is advisable to use an electronic version of the table (available from the book's website), as it makes it easier for updates and to create more space for the information (where needed). Electronic copies can also be more easily distributed around a team. For brevity, our case study example (Table 6.1) shows a selection of purpose targets/design ideas and not the complete set for the whole case study website design.

The first task is to make a list of things that the website should be capable of doing or enabling the user to do. Collectively, this will form the purpose of the website – the combined reasons for its existence. A good starting point is the list of project attributes (defined in Step 1) and the web design requirements list (defined in Step 3) – these are early

Table 6.1: Purpose aspirations table (Step 4)

Purpose Aspirations Table
Website ID: World Religions
Author (form): FK (Weeks 4/5)

ID	Priority Status (1 – 5, 1 = high)	Purpose Targets (List of things website should do or users will be able to do (i.e., reasons for website to exist))	Test result (Y/N)		Ways to Achieve Purpose Targets (design ideas) (Stated design ideas to satisfy each specific purpose target – put prominent ways in bold.)	Test result (Y/N)	Target Date	Done /Date
1	1	Provide info on the main religions – with reasonable depth of description/ explanation for each		1	**Separate pages for each Religion**		Week 8	
				2	Analysis – use reference material		"	
				3	Styles for various ages		"	
2	2	Structured info available		1	**drop menus – each topic**		"	
				2	**Splitting info into clear areas**		"	
				3	Consider word search function		"	
3	4	Ability to contact author		1	Email link		Week 6	
				2	Include 'about us' page		"	
				3				

summaries of the main ambitions of the website. It will probably also help to refer to the various illustrations in Chapter 2, which relate to the development scenarios, user types, and categories of websites. The targeted purpose of a website represents the root justification for making the effort to create and implement the website – its 'reason for being'. Without a clear list of purpose aspirations, it would be difficult and aimless to continue the development project. In the absence of clear and detailed intentions, how could we measure success and recognise if we had achieved the objectives? Each purpose item should be recognisable as an individual purpose (not a combination of separate purposes) and defined in such a way that it is reasonably possible to imagine design ideas that could satisfy the needs. Some initial purposes might be too broad in scale and need to be broken down into smaller units.

Begin by constructing bullet point comments in the 'Purpose Targets' column. Initially this list will be in some kind of random order, but after assigning priorities to the list, you may wish to place your list in order of priority to make it easier to proceed later. It could require several attempts to build up this list of targets and also to decide on priorities – the sessions will involve team discussions, brainstorming, and/or developer–client meetings. It is one of the most important stages in the project and should not be unduly rushed.

Deciding priorities requires consideration of issues specifically related to the project in question, issues that will be a mixture of business, personal, marketing and conceptual in nature. It is often difficult to distinguish between the priority status of some purpose targets, and hence they would be grouped together at the same priority level. The priority level will be useful in making decisions about how much time and effort to spend later on design/implementation/testing for each of the purpose targets. Each of the needs should be specified in the table as concisely as possible so that readability is good and speedy, leading to greater effectiveness when trying to satisfy those design needs.

It is quite possible that this step will be more difficult than you first anticipated. The realisation and determination of all the factual information necessary to completely ascertain the purpose targets of a website, and hence define a website project, can be quite elusive at first. The initial drafts of the documentation might be a little patchy and fragmented, but work with these until something more tangible, comprehensive, and cohesive evolves. Try to use simple language and short bullet point sentences; brevity and clarity will help avoid confusion and enable more speedy reviews and checking later. Once we have a clear list of prioritised targets, we can continue with the remainder of the table, stating detailed design ideas that match purpose targets one by one.

Examples of typical website purposes are as follows:

- Market a product or service
- Provide an opportunity for online sales or a service
- Bridge gap between online store and real-world store(s)
- Provide online support and information
- Increase customer base and awareness
- Entertain
- Amuse or engage
- Gain membership interest/adoption
- Educate/train
- Inform
- Make or provide contact
- Support/help people
- Distribute information
- Enlighten/motivate

This list is quite general, and so for a particular website's purpose aspirations table, it would be worthwhile to use words as specific as possible to that website (i.e., to expand on the list items above so that the purpose target descriptions relate as closely as possible to the particular website being designed). The purpose targets need to be described as briefly as possible so that the table is concise and nicely readable, but at a level of granularity that makes them clear and understandable. Each listed design 'need' has to be clear enough and identifiable enough that distinct design ideas can be derived and checked later to match that need.

Each website that is created on the Web will tend to have a unique main purpose aspiration or combination of purpose aspirations. Where purposes of different websites overlap or seem identical, those websites are in direct competition (for potential audiences and audience time). The competitive edge is gained by careful selection of content and by developing unique, effective, and attractive ways to deliver the targeted purpose(s). Taking care to create good usability and appropriate high-quality aesthetics will help – so, too, will good marketing of the website.

The 'Ways to Achieve Purpose Targets' column has default space for up to three possible ways that the design is to focus on each of the purpose targets. This is a sample number of design ideas, as the actual number of ideas, of course, cannot be predetermined. In some cases, there will only be one or two design ideas that are needed (or can be imagined). In some situations, more than three design ideas will emerge. In this case, simply add rows into the electronic version of the table. The specification of the design ideas is often a very difficult task to fulfil – even if the idea has sprung to mind, it can be tricky to put the idea into succinct words.

For the various sets of design ideas (each associated with a particular target purpose), choose what you believe to be the most significant of those ideas and put it (or them) in bold. This action is helpful in later stages (including review stages) when perhaps having to economise on the number of implementation tasks to be executed in the project – i.e., if the project schedule begins to slip or deadlines have to be altered. Some purpose targets have characteristics that demand complex or multiple design ideas, but a high number of design ideas for a particular purpose target could be indicating that it needs to be broken down into finer points (making new separate purpose targets).

To check for completeness, the only way is (individually or as a team) to 'walk through' each purpose target and associated design ideas to see if you can visualise how this would work in pragmatic terms. This range of required skills may mean that a small group of people are needed to complete this step. When deciding if this step is complete, at least one reasonably strong matching design idea has to be present for each purpose need. A 'need' item cannot be left without a design idea. In addition, all the purpose aspiration 'needs' have to be included in the table. The involvement of user representatives is an important feature of confidently moving on to the next step of the process – e.g., helping to double-check if a complete and contiguous set of design needs and design solutions is represented in the table.

There are two columns in the table that relate to recording test results. These are left blank at this stage, as they become operable during the step that deals with full testing of the implemented website (Step 11). The 'target' and 'done' dates are to help with project management, contributing to the ongoing time and task analysis (introduced in Step 2) – in particular, keeping Gantt charts and milestone charts up to date and deciding if any remedial action is required to keep to the project schedule. At the moment, only the 'target' date is known.

If the table is refined and developed during this and subsequent steps of the process, an archive of previous versions of the table should be stored for possible future reflection and comparison.

Exercises

Seminar Topics

1. To what extent do you think the results of creating the contents of the 'Purpose Targets' column would vary if you concentrated on one only of
    (i) what the website should do; or
    (ii) what the user will be able to do?
2. "I know what needs to be done – there's no point in writing out the bullet points in the table". Analyse and discuss this statement.
3. To what extent do we need to think about characteristics/ expectations of our target audience when completing the work for the purpose aspirations table?

Tutorial Exercises

1. Define, in your own words, what is meant by the phrase 'purpose target'?
2. How many design ideas are needed for each purpose target?
3. How would you utilise the 'target' and 'done' date information with the completion of the time/task analysis documentation?

Case Study

1. Complete a first draft of Column 3 of the purpose aspirations table ('Purpose Targets') using the design documentation from previous steps as a starting point.
2. Place the list of purpose targets into prioritised order.
3. Consider various ways of designing the website to meet the various purpose target needs, and indicate the strongest ideas for each stated need.
4. Apply target dates for each item (making sure they relate to the time/task analysis documentation, initially completed in Step 2 of BWD).

6.2 Step 5: Usability and Aesthetic Requirements Recognition

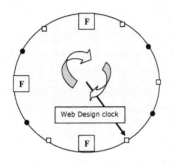

In Chapter 1, we introduced how the key to an effective and successful website is to balance the aesthetic and usability needs around the pivotal purpose needs of the website. Balancing, in this context, means matching the requirements with specially selected design characteristics and giving appropriate emphasis to both usability and aesthetics, centred on the critical aspect of 'purpose'. We have deliberately combined attention to aesthetics and usability in this section rather than deal with them separately, as they extensively intertwine in concept and practice. In the analysis and consideration of either aspect, one often finds that decisions are being made that affect the other aspect. Designers must make sure that they are making design decisions that contribute positively to both aspects and have the overall aim of optimising the presence and power of each of the three characteristics.

In Chapters 3 and 4, respectively, the subjects of usability and aesthetics, in particular relation to website design, are discussed in substantial detail. Neither those chapters nor this section instruct how to make specific design decisions to successfully produce specific sets of usability characteristics or specific aesthetics. For one thing, there is never only one way of arriving at those characteristics, and also the contexts of each situation within which such decisions have to be made vary immensely. The nature of each project, the target user community, and the detailed background behind each component decision vary so extensively that 'cookbook' answers to problems are not relevant. Also, to include a specific list of design ideas for target situations would not be practicable – there are too many genres and types of needs within those genres to attempt to cover. Besides, an important issue is to keep the Web 'alive' by encouraging individuality rather than clones of 'predetermined' detailed designs. Guidance, however, is given on usability concepts and heuristics (in this chapter and in Chapter 3), and the discussion in Chapter 4 adds to guidance later in this chapter to help with the pragmatics of addressing aesthetic design. In short, the BWD methodology is there to support and guide the process and is not designed to replace the skills and imagination of the analyst/designer.

At this stage of design, it is recommended that there be close liaison with users and clients. The involvement of sample target users in usability and aesthetic testing (within Step 11 of BWD) is very beneficial to the project, and so analysis, discussions, and/or surveys with those groups at this early stage have an extra benefit – assisting the making of arrangements for the testing later. It is key at this stage to talk with user/client representatives about their thoughts and preferences regarding the usability and aesthetics of the website – ideas, dislikes, etc.

Usability Considerations

The first decision to make is whether you see your website as being in the 'straight' or 'curved' usability categories. Figures 6.1a–d (reprinted here from illustrations given in Chapter 3) will help in deciding between 'straight' and 'curved' usability categories and will guide you in a general sense with the type of usability characteristics at which to aim. Each case needs to be considered on its own merits, but here is an indicative list of a few typical scenarios:

- Retail website (e.g., household goods, foods, etc.): straight usability
- Traditional corporate organisation website: straight usability
- Pop or other music style 'band' site: curved/straight usability (depends on the nature of the artists and their 'image')
- New media consultancy website: curved/straight usability (depends on the market positioning and subject area)
- Arts/artist website: curved usability
- Cult interest website: curved usability

It is fair to say that for any of the above, an argument to place the example in another usability category could be made. It is not possible or useful to rigidly compartmentalise (especially very early in a project) – the list above is indicative. It is, however, crucial that the categorisation be considered and discussed, as it helps to reveal a great deal about intentions and hopes for the website. If in any doubt for any website, begin with the possibility that curved usability is applicable and move towards 'straightness' if appropriate after analysing the situation in more detail. The label that the site is given by the design team is of little importance in itself in the wider scheme of things – the real importance is in what actually is designed and implemented. The labeling, though, will help guide and influence thought and decisions, but should not fix those choices. For example, in less well defined situations, the adoption of a mixture of the two types as a label draws attention to just that point – that the design decisions will work towards establishing a website identity that relates to both curved and straight usability (i.e., having a *degree* of curvedness).

The guidelines (Figs. 6.1a–d) are based on reworked and extended rationalisations of ideas previously introduced by Jacob Nielsen [1], Muller et al. [2], Steve Krug [3], Jared Spool [4], and John Cato [5], amongst others in this area. This development of the previously published work on usability had the combined aims of

- simplifying and paraphrasing;
- grouping ideas into common areas; and
- expanding the guidelines to accommodate the notions of *curved* and *straight* usability types.

Later in this section, we will go through the structure and completion of the usability planning table documentation. In preparation for being able to tackle that task, let's take a further look at the usability guidelines (Figs. 6.1a–d). The summary guidelines are broken down into four components (content assimilation, navigation, audience awareness, and process) for both straight and curved types of usability.

Consider the information you already have regarding the desired nature and characteristics of your website (by referring to design documentation already completed and the associated reference information provided in Chapter 2). What is the general style and type of website needed? What can we say about the target user community? Consider how this information impacts on the ideal usability characteristics for the website.

First, let's take a look at the 'content assimilation' component (in Fig. 6.1a). Does it seem that simplicity, brevity, and clarity are definitely important features needed in the design? Alternatively, could this style of design detract in any way from one or more of the purposes of the site? It is fairly easy to adopt simplicity and brevity, but not so easy to simultaneously achieve clarity; it involves very careful use of minimal words, images, and layout design to get the essential message across – everything in the right place at the right time to make things easily recognisable, noticed, and understood.

		Straight Usability	Curved Usability
Content Assimilation	1	Simplicity in design is often very successful.	The targeted impact and experience of the website might be of obscurity, abstractedness, challenge, intrigue, and/or chance. This means that the 'traditional' notion of simple, clear, and speedily understood design has to be replaced by one that more appropriately caters for whatever 'curved usability' impact and experience are desired.
	2	Brevity and clarity are like gold dust.	
	3	Website content is *glanced at*, not carefully and slowly studied and read.	
	4	Choices (links/selections) available to website users should be designed with speed and impatience in mind.	

Fig. 6.1a: Usability guidelines analysis

The popular theory is that people who visit websites always require that the content can be read and understood in a speedy fashion. In many cases, this is true – for example, checking the availability and cost of a specific retail item. The aspirations of our website might, though, be such that a more challenging and 'engaging' style is needed for the layout (i.e., some degree of 'curved' usability). Perhaps even some retail sites would benefit from a nonstraight usability approach – depending on the products and the clientele. The navigation structure, appearance, and working characteristics are key to presenting the nature of the website itself. We know that in most cases website users like speed of navigation and can get impatient if they get lost or take a wrong route. However, the opposite of the 'fast fix' might be what you as a designer are striving for: to provide quite a different experience for your website users (e.g., to present challenges or provoke thought or action).

Incidentally, it is often the small details that gain a very positive user reaction. For example, the detailed graphics, text, or image style (e.g., for navigation buttons) – i.e., its appropriateness and attractiveness – is at least as important as whether or not the navigation uses frames, pull-down menus, or smart scripting/interactivity, etc. At this point, we are treading into the world of aesthetics, which is an example of why usability and aesthetics need to be contemplated and designed in close proximity.

		Straight Usability	Curved Usability
Navigation	5	Comfortable (easy choices and recognition) plus speedy navigation around the website is is desirable.	Navigation ease and awareness of position within the total map of the site might be something that needs to be made 'less comfortable', more thoughtful, not quite so 'immediate', and perhaps more 'conceptual' to match the desired website style and character.
	6	Well-chosen (unambiguous, brief, relevant, true) words and an understandable layout of visuals and text are vital.	
	7	Presenting a complete view of a site and current location in that context at any time the user is moving around a site is a fundamental navigation component.	
	8	Clear navigation is *at least* as important as the quality of the content material.	
	9	The 'virtual' world of a website suffers in navigation terms unless you can manage to 'plant' landmarks in some way and represent the 'bigger picture'.	

Fig. 6.1b: Usability guidelines analysis

Figure 6.1b addresses specifically issues relating to navigation. Depending on the details of the website being designed, making choices on how content is to be accessed and how to organise interactivity and navigation might be quite challenging. The site may need total 'comfort', total 'unease', or something in between. As a designer, you need to know enough about the purpose targets and the audience to determine the nature of the usability required.

To help place the type of usability targeted at the right level of straightness and curvedness, it can be useful to reflect on design documentation completed earlier (e.g., website design context framework, website scenario statement, website design requirements list, website genre/subtypes, website user characteristics) and reference material such as 'website design feature trends' (all covered in previous chapters). The categorisation and trends details can be used to indicate suitable candidate usability design ideas. This can be combined with information gained from discussions directly with clients and with any potential target users. These studies help, but it is not possible for them alone to lead to detailed and specific design decisions. That largely relies on the skills and experience of the designer(s). It is important that the fine details of how the usability characteristics are defined are based on decisions and ideas formed at a personal level. This is how designs become unique and original and hence spark the interest and engagement of the website user.

The level of 'usability comfort' is a characteristic that can also be associated with the aesthetic qualities of a website. Usability therefore again is impacting on the aesthetics. Awareness and consideration of connections between aesthetics and usability are helpful in forming the context for deciding on the usability features of the website pages.

In addition to being concerned about site navigation, we must also take care in designing local navigation so that awareness is heightened in terms of the suitability (in terms of the website design intentions) of where to look and move to around a particular page or section of a site.

The terminology, expressions, and detailed visual content ('local navigation') need to be appropriate for the website's target purpose(s) and have layout/interactivity characteristics that make the content usable. Great content that goes unnoticed or is not suitably accessible by the website user is wasted content. In many cases, a website benefits from having the design present a clear contextual view of the sitemap (straight usability). However, it may not be desirable to do so – the main purpose and aims of the site might mean that a nontraditional view is taken on the transparency of the site context (curved usability). The designer has to consider if it makes good sense to the central purposes of the site to make the overall view and awareness of the whole site (i.e., what is there, where it is, and why it is there) immediately apparent to the visitor. An alternative approach might be to make the site user 'work' for that knowledge – perhaps a little like typical 'action' video games. In other words, the process and style of website navigation can be used to contribute to the conceptual experience. In extreme cases, navigation for a curved usability website could be quite obscure and/or emotive.

To 'plant' landmarks in a website, to represent the 'bigger picture' (and hence replicate the advantages that we enjoy in the 'real world'), is a usability aspect that often remains unsolved in typical website designs. In the 'real' world, we take (sometimes subconsciously) note of our surroundings en route to a particular location or goal (for example, for driving a car, moving around a large store, etc.). Partly due to the capability of quickly 'transporting' to any points on the Web by a few simple clicks of a mouse button, we can very quickly get disoriented and don't normally get the chance to see any 'surroundings' on the way from A to B. If you were to take time out in your design work to find how this problem can be offset, even by some degree, by thoughtful and innovative design, then you would be significantly furthering the quality of your website and of the art of website usability design in general.

The usability guidelines expressed in Fig. 6.1c relate to audience awareness – of a site's content and how to access that content, and our awareness of the audience. Please note that all these points apply equally for straight and curved types of usability. Audience awareness of what is offered is crucial to maximising access and use of whatever the website provides. The successful design aimed at achieving this is helped by good awareness of the audience (characteristics, needs, etc.) and their ongoing interactions with the website.

A key point to bear in mind is that we as designers must take the initiative in being creative and determined to attract the interest of potential audiences – as there is no automatic reason for anyone to use the site, we have to earn their interest. It needs to be very evident to the prospective user that their time spent will be worthwhile. One thing to remember is that although time has to be invested to evolve a good usability design, it takes approximately the same time to develop and test the code for a bad design as it does for a good design, and bad designs are very damaging financially and productively. So, attention to detail in making the implemented designs appropriate is worth that effort.

Figure 6.1c refers to the 'homepage', which plays an important part in creating effective audience awareness. The homepage is the main anchor page of a website and is usually the page seen when the site is first opened (although many sites have a short video/animation style item that runs immediately prior to the homepage).

There is a great deal written elsewhere about the design of homepages [3], with the main points being to use the homepage to clearly establish the nature, purpose, scope, and operation of your website, using a mixture of appropriately chosen visuals and text descriptions and clues.

Straight and Curved Usability		
Audience Awareness	10	Homepages are special – they are the equivalent of the shop window, the front page of a newspaper, the opening scene in a film, the news headlines, or the front cover, and hence good presence of an item here almost guarantees user awareness and attention.
	11	Keep the site fresh, accurate, relevant, and up-to-date to keep the interest of the audience alive, and react promptly to any invited (audience) interaction.
	12	Web users are fantastically varied, with unique reactions and characteristics, so audience identification and analysis helps, but complex human nature has to be catered for.
	13	Users are not obliged to care about or like our websites; *we* have to trigger and nurture that attraction.
	14	Good (usable) webpages are like good road signs and good billboard adverts, so observing how *they* work is worthwhile research.

Fig. 6.1c: Usability guidelines analysis

The homepage is where everyone served by the site wants a prominent presence. In a project that involves designing a website to cover the needs of several different departments, groups, or individuals, it is with the design of the homepage that the website designer can definitely experience the taste and responsibilities of power! Everyone wants a prominent position on the homepage, the strongest presentation, and the most interesting links and interactivity. Give a long look to options and possibilities. Is it possible to satisfy everyone and everything? Are compromises needed? Are there possible adverse effects on overall clarity and the desired aesthetics? Some decisions may need to be made by someone other than the designer (a clear project team structure and hierarchy helps to smoothly handle this situation).

The homepage of any site is crucially important. The desired characteristics and flavours of usability and aesthetics need to be communicated so that the user very quickly has the best chance of being attracted to and staying with the site. Constant attention is needed after implementation to keep the website 'alive' by freshening the look and the content regularly. Reactions to user feedback and queries also need to be given promptly and carefully. Thoroughly consider how users are invited to make contact and with whom. The usability style of the homepage sets the scene for how the user is likely to perceive the whole site. When reflecting on how effective the design of a homepage (and other page types) might be, consider how it might compare with good road signs, TV/billboard advertising, and/or posters for concert shows. To learn how the most successful of these are constructed and operate would be a significant help in the task of designing our websites. Does website design swiftly and efficiently tell everyone about everything every time? Does it secure interest in making the next step (in this case to stay with the site and access at least some of the content)? Does the website 'compete' well with competition only a glance away?

Clearly, there are identifiable audiences for specific sites, and it is well worth spending time building up profiles of those groups. Knowledge and awareness of tastes and preferences will help enormously with your design task. Human nature is complex, however, and not easily predictable.

		Straight and Curved Usability	
Process	15	Testing (including one or more cycles of user testing) for usability is extremely important – begin it early in the project.	
	16	Planning, design, and an iterative process are very important features in deriving effective usability characteristics.	

Fig. 6.1d: Usability guidelines analysis

Figure 6.1d refers to usability guidelines that relate to the process of the implementation project. The recommendations apply equally for straight and curved usability scenarios.

The formal comprehensive testing and evaluation stage (aesthetics, usability, and purpose) is in Step 11. However, testing should be an ongoing process throughout the project. If the ethos of testing (ideas, prototypes, and approaches) is infused at every stage of the project, this will help optimise the final result. The earlier that problems are identified and resolved, the sooner that effectiveness can be established and strengthened. The later that difficulties and gaps in requirements come to the surface, the more costly and time consuming it is to recover. It would be unusual to resolve all usability needs and challenges on the first attempt. Therefore we need to give careful attention to usability at each planning, design, and implementation phase – review and react to usability issues on an iterative basis, revisiting them until satisfactorily resolved.

The usability guidelines recognise the importance of a structured process incorporating planning, design, and iteration. This places the quest for appropriate usability into a context of rigour and comprehensiveness.

Usability – Specifying Design

It is the usability planning table (Table 6.2a,b) that provides the opportunity to use the outcomes of analysis based on issues raised in the previous section and characterise in detail the usability design of the website. This acts as a tool of the design itself and as a method of documenting the design decisions made. Table 6.2a shows some example target usability features for a website relating to our case study. There are only three target usability characteristics in this example table, but for most websites there would be a greater number present. The first column to complete is column 3 – 'Target Usability for this Website'. The requirement here is to make a list of usability features that are relevant to the website being designed. There are many usability features that exist in the world of software interface design and several that consistently apply to the various genres and types of websites. Try to note down as many aspects of usability as possible that you feel have some relevance and importance to the particular project website. Some will be generally applicable to most websites, and others will be specific and unique to your website (it is the usability characteristics that have a degree of unique identifiability that will help make the website itself unique). Examples might be 'to use easily recognisable visual clues for navigation', 'consistency of choice selection approaches', or 'user navigation recognisably needing pattern matching/problem solving'.

An analysis of the list that you have made may result in refinements to phrases and terminology and perhaps items removed, added, or broken down into separate subitems. It is important for wording to be such that all team members involved understand and recognise the usability need expressed. Clear, concise, and focussed usability targets will help to identify clearly associated design ideas later. Make repeated reflections on the purpose aspirations table and the web requirements list, so that the documentation matches up well. There is no limit to the number of target usability needs, although typically there might be 5–6.

Table 6.2a: Usability planning table – Step 5

Usability Planning Table				Comments:			
Website ID: World Religions **Author (form):** FK (Weeks 4/5)							
ID	**Priority Status**	**Target Usability for this Website**	Test result (Y/N)	**Design Ideas to Achieve the Desired Usability Features**	Test result (Y/N)	**Target Date**	**Done/Date**
	1–5 (1 is highest)	List of usability features and attributes *particularly* desired for this site		Briefly describe website design ideas (two or three at least for each target need, with prominent ways in **bold**).			
1	1	Site should offer clear navigation tools and make user aware of current location	1				
			2				
			3				
2	2	Site should offer readability, clarity, and relevance	1				
			2				
			3				
			4				
3	3	Site should be consistent	1				
			2				

Table 6.2b: Usability planning table – Step 5

Usability Planning Table
Website ID: World Religions
Author (form): FK (Weeks 4/5)

Comments:

ID	Priority Status 1–5 (1 is highest)	Target Usability for this Website	Test result (Y/N)	Design Ideas to Achieve the Desired Usability Features (Briefly describe website design ideas (two or three at least for each target need, with prominent ways in **bold**).	Test result (Y/N)	Target Date	Done/ Date
1	1	Site should offer clear navigation tools and make user aware of current location		1 Offer user control and choice of location by use of buttons/links		Week 7	
				2 Status bar display at each page. Consider 'breadcrumbs'			
				3 Clearly labelled pages			
2	2	Site should offer readability, clarity, and relevance		1 Use of regular clear headings, font size, and colour		Week 7	
				2 Use short blocked paragraphs dealing with specific topics			
				3 Use 'white space' breaks and sections			
				4 Use visual clues (e.g., icons/images)			
3	3	Site should be consistent		1 Buttons and menu options same on every page		Week 6	
				2 Page layout and structure uniform and consistent			

The next task is to prioritise the list of usability needs (numbering each of them 1 to 5 in Column 2). This prioritising is useful in that it indicates how much relative effort and attention are needed for the later design and implementation tasks.

Once you are happy with the prioritised list of usability needs, and especially if you are using an electronic version of the documentation (available via the book's website), you may wish to reformat the table so that the design targets are now placed in prioritised order. We need to return to the usability planning table to allocate design ideas for each target usability need, but we will do this later, as it is more productive if this is done in conjunction with deriving the design for aesthetic needs. It helps to combine this task with that of usability, as the two very often impact and relate to each other. So, to be able to make usability and aesthetic design decisions in parallel or at least in close proximity makes sense. For example, a designer might come up with several potential usability design options, each with varying aesthetic consequences, and hence the best usability design options are those that positively feed into the aesthetic needs of the website. Hence, the next task is to establish the aesthetic needs for the site.

Considering Aesthetics

What sells a car? The engine size, acceleration, the drink holder, boot space? Or is it the colour, the upholstery, the comfort, the smell of new leather, or the sound? What attracts the website user to spend time with and return to a website? The content, the speed of access, the range of options? Or is it the style, the ambience, the mood, or the attitude?

It is difficult to say, except that it is almost always likely to be some type of mixture of the key purpose, usability and aesthetic characteristics, depending on the context, the person, and the situation. So, as designers, we are looking to create a suitable set of design ideas that address a balanced set of identified website needs, optimising effectiveness and potential.

At this stage, we hope to have analysed and fully understood the purpose and usability requirements of the website, and now we need to think carefully about the aesthetics of the website. What impression are we trying to make? What feeling are we trying to induce? Are we trying to portray a particular attitude, ambience, and style? All of these should be relevant and support the overall purpose of the website and associate closely with the characteristics and expectations of the expected audience community.

Aesthetics is a very personal thing and a very human thing. We need to treat it with care and respect and not assume or presume. The main duty we have as website designers is to establish and recognise what aesthetic is required for our particular project website. To do this is essential. It is achieved by initially thinking about the website purpose/usability needs and anticipating the expectations of the target users and discussing aesthetic possibilities directly with clients. Some websites will have clear target communities with identifiable characteristics and preferences, but of course there will be some situations where it is not so straightforward to form a picture.

The approach to establishing good aesthetic design follows a pattern similar to that of determining good usability design. It is necessary to

- identify the aesthetic needs,
- prioritise the aesthetic needs,
- associate specific design ideas with each aesthetic need, and
- use project management techniques to monitor and control achievement of the target designs.

Table 6.3a shows the aesthetics planning table for use in designing the desired aesthetic and documenting that design information. There is an important point here: as with all the design documentation utilised, the aesthetics planning table is not there simply to record factual design information but also to help with the *process* of the design work. In other words, the act of thinking through what is needed to complete the various columns of the table becomes the vehicle for analysing, understanding, and designing the aesthetic qualities of the site – the documentation provides a focus and a framework for the creative work. The examples in Table 6.3a are target aesthetics for a particular project design and continue our case study example project.

To identify desired aesthetic characteristics for a website is not an easy task, as although we tend to readily recognise if an aesthetic is inappropriate, it is not so easy for us to *predict* what aesthetic is going to fit a particular design situation. There are many complexities involved in this area, and Chapter 4 discusses aesthetics and gives some guidance. Take another look if you need help placing your project website into the wider context and help in commencing this difficult and intriguing task. Developers will undoubtedly need the help of user/client representatives in identifying and deriving an understanding and appreciation of the aesthetics that would be most suitable for the website.

Budgets and plans need to take into account the time and energy needed for this phase of a website design project. It is important to allow enough time and allocate people with the best skills to be studying and ascertaining the usability and aesthetic needs – and to have the same personnel looking at both aspects if at all possible.

For designers and/or design teams that are not very experienced (and/or a project website that does not have easily defined needs for usability and aesthetics), a good approach is to gather the project team together and surf through a variety of existing websites. Make sure the range is wide and includes examples of sites within and slightly outside of the genre of your project website. Encourage everyone to make comments about the sites that you look at – comments about the mood, the impression, the feel, the ambience, ease of use, navigation familiarity, etc. Once it is clear that people are recognising and verbalising the usability and aesthetics of the sites visited, move the discussion on to 'whether particular characteristics witnessed would be good or not-so-good for your project website'. Make sure someone is taking notes (or, even better, videorecord the session) because the results provided will form vital input to the task of making analysis/design decisions for your own project website.

The analysis of the aesthetic possibilities and desires has to be crystallised into a stated set of target aesthetic characteristics specifically for your project website, to be placed into the aesthetics planning table (an example can be seen in Table 6.3a, which relates to our case study). The table has a structure and format similar to both the purpose aspirations and the usability planning tables, which helps when reflecting on and reviewing it for consistency and completeness.

It is usual to begin with Column 3 – to list the aesthetic needs of the website. It works best to use bullet form or short notes (for ease of reading and encouraging a focus on salient issues). Once a complete list of needs has been placed on the form, the next phase is to consider the prioritisation of the individual needs – use Column 2 to assign a hierarchy of aesthetic needs (giving '1' for a high priority status through to '5' for a low priority status). It is a piece of information that will be useful later in the project if you have to choose between implementation options or decide on the time to be spent implementing each design component.

Table 6.3a: Aesthetics planning table – Step 5

Aesthetics Planning Table
Website ID: World Religions
Author (form): FK (Week 5)

Comments:

ID	Priority Status (1–5, 1 = highest)	Target Aesthetic Characteristics (List of the feelings, moods, and impressions to be created by the site/pages)	Test result (Y/N)		Design Ideas to Achieve the Desired Usability Features (Briefly describe the aesthetic design ideas (two or three for each target need, with prominent ways in **bold**).	Test result (Y/N)	Target Date	Done/ Date
1	1	Site should be warm and welcoming		1				
				2				
				3				
2	2	Calm and straight-forward		1				
				2				
				3				
3	2	Neutral impression						

Table 6.3b: Aesthetics planning table – Step 5

Aesthetics Planning Table Website ID: World Religions Author (form): FK (Week 5)			Comments:				
ID	Priority Status	Target Aesthetic Characteristics	Test result (Y/N)	Design Ideas to Achieve the Desired Usability Features	Test result (Y/N)	Target Date	Done/ Date
	1–5 (1 = highest)	List, of the feelings, moods, and impressions to be created by the site/pages		Briefly describe the aesthetic design ideas (two or three for each target need, with prominent ways in **bold**).			
1	1	Site should be warm and welcoming		1 **Colours – fresh/warm choice**		Week 8	
				2 Consistent and 'open' layout			
				3 **Inviting language**			
2	2	Calm and straight-forward		1 **Avoid clutter and gimmicks**		Week 8	
				2 Small range of colours/objects			
				3 Keep focus on clarity/education			
3	2	Neutral impression		1 **Take care not to 'colour code' religions (subliminal)**		Week 8	
				2 Consistency in headings/layout			
				3 Avoid emotive/loaded expression			

As with the usability planning table, it is good practice to sort the aesthetics table so that the higher-priority items are at the top of the list (simply for ease of recognition of the order).

Now that prioritised usability and prioritised aesthetic needs have been clearly and fully specified, it is time to work on identifying design ideas for each specified need.

Usability and Aesthetics – Establishing Design Ideas

As the notions of usability and aesthetics are so entwined and interdependent, the most pragmatic and effective approach is to work on developing the design ideas for both sets of specification needs (usability and aesthetics) in parallel. If it is a team project, it could be split between two designers or groups of designers. If it is an individual project, then it is a matter of dividing and allocating time to interchange between the two areas. As each usability design idea emerges, consider if the use of the idea would positively or negatively impact the aesthetics of the site, and vice versa. Inevitably, compromises will need to be made and some impacts and influences will only become fully apparent when implemented and tested. Hence, a prototyping and flexible approach is needed, coupled with a sensitivity to the complexities of the human response to the details of a design (interface functionality and operational characteristics) and the reaction to the experience of using that design. When working on a project, the choice has to be made between starting with usability or aesthetic ideas; the selection will largely depend on whichever seems to have the clearer objectives and/or solutions. The initial design elements for one of the two areas will almost certainly help clarify the way forward when there is any uncertainty about the other area.

For the purposes of this book, let's presume that the project begins by looking at the usability design ideas to match the usability needs already identified.

In a typical website design project, a single usability need might be satisfied with one or more of perhaps several design ideas – it is not the case that there is only one way of achieving a given usability need. In one way this is good – it means that we have a wide range of possibilities from which to choose, making it more likely that we will develop a unique identity of the website design. Conversely, it also means that, as designers, we have to *make* choices. In most cases, we will implement two or more ideas per target need, so, in the table (Table 6.3b), we note down the details of what we recognise as the main and secondary design ideas for each usability need. Those ideas that we feel are the preferred or strongest ideas can be represented in bold. This serves purely as a reminder, when implementing the various designs, of which design ideas demand special attention. Often, we will actually implement more than one technique for achieving a usability need, and in other cases we will select only one – perhaps if the project time available for implementation work becomes reduced, for example. However, the latter approach carries with it the risk of not fully satisfying a usability need – i.e., if the idea doesn't work as well as we would expect.

There is no fixed way of targeting a particular usability need. For usability design ideas, as with aesthetic design ideas, one of the best ways to compile a personal checklist of possible options is to take some time to surf and analyse existing websites. Select websites in the genre of your project and/or websites that you feel are likely to exhibit the usability features also required as characteristics of your project website. You will probably find at least some examples of designs that you admire and can utilise, and it will help formulate a better understanding of what works and what doesn't work.

Table 6.3b shows some example usability design ideas (based on our case study) specified for a particular set of design needs. The aim is to keep the descriptions of the ideas simple and concise and to try and ensure that each idea represents a single recognisable design feature and not a complex combination of features. Where several design ideas are specified for a particular target characteristic (two or three design needs is usually optimum), you could highlight any ideas that you feel are particularly important or strong.

The date columns in the usability planning table are particularly useful in medium to large projects, but feel free to use timescales appropriate to your project (e.g., date, week no., time of day, etc.).

Utilising estimated and actual task completion dates introduces a useful layer of 'checks and balances' to the design task. It helps avoid allowing any of the usability needs and design solutions to be missed and/or to be implemented so late that they slow down future stages of the project. Refer back to the outcomes of Step 2 (e.g., to the milestone chart, and CPA/Gantt charts if you constructed them) to be sure that your timescale plans fit in with overall project planning scheduling.

In order to complete the final column of the table ('Done /Date' – a tick to say it is done, plus the date), it is necessary later to review progress. To an extent, this can be done at any time during the project, but most likely it will be carried out in the R&R steps.

In parallel with setting out usability design ideas, we need to address the task of identifying aesthetic design ideas. The approach to conceiving them is similar to that of usability design ideas – using your own design skills, referring to previous design work examples (e.g., for websites in the same genre), and being sensitive to requirements and design details already established for this website prior to this step. In addition, we have the benefit of our emerging usability design work, which directly leads to ideas for aesthetic design. It is advisable to spend some time alongside user/client representatives when discussing and/or evaluating prototype ideas for aesthetics design.

It is very beneficial to spend some time 'inventing' new ways to achieve better aesthetic designs (compared with using ideas you've already seen on the Web or the ones you have used previously). This will help build up a resource base of design ideas. Reflect on what your website (and/or individual pages) is trying to achieve in terms of emotions and experience and reflect on your own experience and ideas of how visual, sonic, and interactivity characteristics can contribute to that ideal appropriate aesthetic. It is a very good investment to allow the consideration and experimentation of what might at first appear to be very 'offbeat' ideas for aesthetic design. Try them. Test them. See if they work, and if they work well. It can prove to be very painful (eventually) to ignore possible 'great ideas' and not too burdensome at this early stage to spend some time experimenting. This notion of experimentation time of course has to be tailored to the available time for the whole project – i.e., if deadlines and budgets are short, then there is a smaller amount of time for research and exploration. Try to remember the 'triangle' – purpose, usability, and aesthetics. We need all three to be of high quality and relevance to produce a balanced and effective website design, and so time spent on each aspect has to be balanced accordingly.

The design ideas are placed in column 6 of Table 6.3b, describing how the design of the website is to relate specifically to each of the aesthetic needs of the website. This aspect can be quite difficult, and it might take some time to get ideas crystallised adequately (or perhaps understand the needs sufficiently) in order to arrive at design features that support and enable the various needs identified. The aesthetic planning table (see the example in Table 6.3b) provides initial space for three ideas per target need. In some cases, there will only be one or maybe two ideas that are relevant. Where there are more than three ideas to document, use the electronic version of the form to make extra space. The space per item on the form is deliberately restricted, as it is more useful (for the design process) to have speed-readable points that are succinct and precise rather than expansive text passages. If one or more of the ideas are recognised as preferable and/or predicted to be more effective, then put them in bold on the form (for ease of recognition later). Longer explanations and discussions for any of the bullet points can be attached on additional sheets if necessary, but remember that brief and clear documentation is more likely to be used in the implementation stages and beyond.

Frequently during the process of setting out aesthetic design bullet points, cross-refer to the usability design work (i.e., the usability planning table) to check for cohesion and any impacts/conflicts.

The date columns are important for reviewing progress later and for planning the resources and activities necessary to complete the various aesthetic designs. Refer back to the plan, timescales, and budget for the whole project at this point to ensure correlation between detailed planning and overall project planning.

In both tables 6.3a and 6.3b, remove or resolve any gaps, conflicts, and repetition, and make clear and precise any vagueness. Both tables need to be sufficiently clear, consistent, and comprehensive that they will be directly useful in subsequent stages – e.g., detailed design of the navigation, screen layouts, content, style, structure, etc.

At this point, you should be feeling quite confident, relieved, and optimistic: confident at arriving at an important phase in the design project and in the knowledge that you have been very thorough in analysing and specifying the requirements and key design features for the project; relieved at completing what at first might have been a rather daunting design task and understanding the scope and depth of what is needed in the remainder of the project; and optimistic that the website project now has a good chance of being very effective and successful, and also enjoyable to develop and implement.

Exercises

Seminar Topics

1. Discuss the similarities and differences between website aesthetics and aesthetics of a home, a pair of shoes, a mobile phone, and a professional football team kit.
2. To what extent can we achieve good website usability without attempting to achieve good website aesthetics (and vice versa)?
3. It is often said that good website usability is defined as "easy to navigate and simple to use". Discuss what this means, and if you feel that this definition is always applicable.

Tutorial Exercises

1. What items of documentation need to be completed in this step (Step 5), and what are the best input sources?
2. What is the best action for a designer if the required usability and/or aesthetic characteristics (i.e., the 'needs') are not immediately apparent?
3. What is the point of the 'Date' and the 'Priority' columns on the usability and aesthetic tables documented in this step?

Case Study

1. Make a list of all the aesthetic and usability characteristics that you would like to implement as part of the design of your case study website. For each one, make a note of why that feature is important.
2. Surf the web to find some websites in the same genre as your case study website. Compare and contrast the aesthetic and usability designs of your website to those of the sites located.
3. Fully complete the usability and aesthetic planning tables for your website project.
4. Apply target dates for each item (making sure they relate to the time/task analysis documentation, – initially completed in Step 2 of BWD).

6.3 Step 6: Review and Reflect (1)

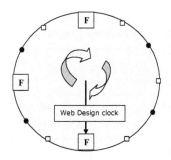

In 'BWD clock' terms, we have reached 6 o'clock – halfway through the cycle of BWD steps – our first chance to formally review and reflect on progress and effectiveness and identify any difficulties to address. This is the first of three 'Review and Reflect' (R&R) steps in the project at which we can take 'flashbacks' to any earlier steps as needed. The flashbacks are so that we can go through one or more previous steps again to resolve a problem or deficiency revealed in the R&R step, producing a new iteration of the design. We then return to the R&R step, and if things are satisfactory we can continue with subsequent steps.

Website design and implementation is clearly a complex operation, even for the simplest of websites, and there is too much at stake, too much detailed information, and too many intricate tasks to work through without any pauses for reflection. To review and reflect on any project is in fact a vital ingredient to success – reviewing progress, decisions, and plans, and reflecting on requirements, possibilities, and constraints.

The scheduled steps for this Review and Reflect activity are placed strategically in the project cycle to try and make them most relevant and worthwhile, providing clear focal points during the project.

Each of these steps has the purpose of studying and evaluating requirements, decisions, designs, and design ideas, plus any related issues that urgently need to be resolved. The precise information and issues that will require attention partly depend on which of the three Review and Reflect steps is in progress – i.e., they depend on the stage reached in the project. The following are likely aspects for study in this first R&R step:

- completeness of 'design needs' specification (purpose, usability, and aesthetics);
- design ideas and their suitability in practical implementation terms and in terms of matching requirements;
- project plan (deadlines, costs, and problems) – check suitability, progress, and accuracy of the Gantt and milestone

charts (and any other project management documentation you use, such as critical path analysis charts);

- recognition of project successes and any knowledge dissemination needs across the team;
- user–developer communication and integration issues;
- identification of any further decisions or information urgently needed and/or proving difficult to resolve or ascertain.

This first 'Review and Reflect' step is quite a special one. It is the 'pause for breath' after the initial analysis and design groundwork and before embarking on the detailed design and implementation stages of the project. We have made a project plan, identified the overall ambitions and aspirations for the project, defined the specific purpose, usability, and aesthetic needs, and proposed design ideas relevant to each of those needs. We must now go through this formal 'checking and assessment' BWD step before continuing with more detailed design (screen layouts, navigation, screen dialogues, purpose maps, etc.), followed by coding and implementation. Small and speedy items can be addressed immediately, but more sizeable problems may need us to metaphorically wind the clock back and reiterate a complete previous step. In BWD, we refer to this action as a 'flashback'.

Subsequent steps of the project (Step 7 onwards) should not be commenced until everyone is sufficiently happy with the outcomes and deliverables of the previous steps. It is an inescapable fact that in any software development project, early correction or resolution of design flaws or omissions leads to greater robustness and effectiveness. Poor or incomplete designs will be revealed at some point and in some way, and if this happens in the latter stages of a project, recovery is likely to be very costly in both time and resources.

Therefore, a substantial amount of time and energy should be invested in this and other R&R steps. All of the BWD documentation, and hence all of the outcomes of each step, have to be studied for completeness and cohesiveness. In isolation, each item has been checked at least once already (when first completed), and several items have already been used in conjunction with each other, but this is a chance to do the checking in the context of the complete project and of project work completed so far.

The procedure for completing R&R checking in BWD comprises a mixture of

- individual analysis,

- group discussion and analysis, and
- team reporting and study of project documentation.

The 'role-playing' structure of the project (established in Step 1) will help determine who should take responsibility for problems and issues that need special attention and deciding which website aspects must be given attention before completion is achieved. To help formalise the outcomes of this step, and to make it easier for future tracking of findings and actions, the outcomes should be documented (see Table 6.4 for an R&R report template and some example reporting based on our case study).

Some problems will be of a nature that still allows progress to the next step, with the problems flagged to be addressed as part of one of the subsequent steps. If so, remember to 'sign-off' those problems later (on the R&R report) as resolved/addressed. The R&R report table (Table 6.4) helps to organise the information so that the 'problems' are clearly identified, the required or completed action is detailed, and its completion is able to be monitored.

Table 6.4: R&R report

Item	Source	Comments / Action	Successfully Resolved Date and Solution
Navigation	Usability table	Alternatives re: menus, frames?	Week 6: frames + JavaScript menu
Colours (back-ground)	Aesthetics table	Associations of colours?	Week 5: experiment with range of pastel colours
Search function	Purpose table	Include or not?	Week 6: focus on good navigation – no searching

R&R Report	
Project name:	World Religions
Direct input (documentation):	usability/aesthetics/purpose tables
BWD step: (6, 9, or 12):	6 (Weeks 5/6)

The 'Item' column should state simply the specific aspect that has been identified as not yet being completed or unsatisfactorily completed. The 'Source' column is used to indicate which particular piece of design documentation was being studied when the problem became apparent (and/or that normally defines or records the item in question).

The 'Comments/Action' column needs to clearly define the problem or difficulty and state possible action (if known). The final column is used to record successful resolution of the issue. Usually this will be required before continuing with subsequent steps, or it could be done later if the problem is not crucial to progressing with the project.

Individuals or small groups who have the responsibility to address the problem item need to use whatever information and resources are available. Information could be from existing design documentation and/or from further analysis of the situation – perhaps with the help of clients or users of the website. In some cases, it might be deemed that particular items cannot be resolved (or that it is not cost/time-efficient to do so). The 'Comments' column has to record this if this is so, and also the extent to which the project is likely to be affected. In extreme cases, project plans and aspirations may need to be reorganised. Very serious problems could even mean that the project has to end or be postponed, which underlines the importance of this step.

Exercises

Seminar Topics

1. Do you think there should be team members dedicated to reviewing the project, or that it should be a shared task by members also involved with other project tasks?
2. What kind of situations (if any) do you think might result in a project being totally halted/cancelled due to the outcomes of a Review and Reflect stage?
3. "Some website projects don't really need any formal 'Review' steps." Discuss.

Tutorial Exercises

1. What is a 'flashback?
2. Name at least three aspects that are reviewed in an R&R step.
3. How is it decided who takes responsibility for resolving particular problems identified in this step?

Case Study

1. Make a list of items and aspects that have been produced, created, or decided so far in your website design project.
2. After reviewing all related items, place the details of any aspects that possibly are incomplete or have problems into a BWD 'Review and Reflect' report form. Make a note of your intended action.
3. Take the action required to look into the problems highlighted and further complete the report form once you (and/or others on your team) have resolved or formed conclusions on each item.

Chapter References

1. Nielsen J. (1994), "Heuristic Evaluation". In J. Nielsen and R.L. Mack (Eds.), *Usability Inspection Methods*, John Wiley & Sons, New York, pp. 25–62.
2. Krug S. (2000), *Don't Make Me Think*, New Riders, Indianapolis
3. Muller M.J., Matheson L., Page C., Gallup R. (1998), "Methods & Tools: Participatory Heuristic Evaluation", *Interactions Archive*, Volume 5, Issue 5, Sept./Oct. 13–18.
4. Jared Spool Interviews:
    http://www.uservision.co.uk/Articles/jaredspool.htm
    (Interview with Jared Spool, *Interfaces Magazine*, British HCI Group, Aug. 2002)
    http://www.usabilitynews.com/news/article432.asp
    (Feature: "Jared Spool, A Man with a Task", May7 2002)
5. Cato J. (2001), *User-Centred Web Design*, Addison-Wesley, Reading, MA.

CHAPTER SEVEN

Designing the Solution

Overview

This chapter deals with some of the key detailed components and steps in the detailed design of a website. It follows on from the previous steps in which purpose, aesthetic, and usability issues were identified and design ideas were formulated and checked.

In this current step, the aim is to derive a navigation design, details of webpage layouts and interface design, plus complete lists of content for the website and constructed 'purpose maps'. The chapter works with several items of documentation to establish the structural and navigation design of the website, screen layouts, and the user/webpage dialogue design. An index of all the website contents is built up (for use as a general reference and as a 'material acquisition' checklist) and 'purpose maps' constructed, which are series of actions for users to follow to achieve each target website purpose.

In this chapter, there is also the second of the Review & Reflect steps, where the created design information is studied and reviewed to confirm whether everything is satisfactory or if further work is needed before progressing. Each of the three steps in this chapter is concluded with seminar, tutorial, and case study exercise – designed to help reinforce and increase understanding of BWD and to help you make practical progress with your own case study project. This chapter includes examples showing how to use the documentation.

Give and Gain

If you give time to this chapter (let's say 65 minutes or so, plus additional time to reinforce understanding using seminar and tutorial questions and obtain practical experience via case study work), this is what you will gain:

- an understanding of how the details of the navigation and interface/layout design can be derived and documented in preparation for actual coding and building;
- an appreciation of how previous requirements acquisition and design preparation can be used to inform detailed design;
- how to use a contents index to ensure complete material acquisition and purpose mapping to cross-check how all target purposes are satisfied;
- practical experience, via case study work, in completing design tasks described and illustrated in the chapter.

7.1 Step 7: Technical Options/Selections

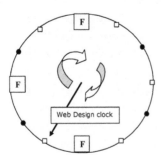

It's 7 o'clock in terms of our 'web design time'. This step heralds the beginning of the detailed design stage, which immediately precedes the steps for building, testing, and evaluating. It is at this point that we should take stock of all the various technical options we have available with regard to developing and implementing the website.

In advance of commencing the design of the website, there will have been some consideration of technical options and issues (see Chapter 2), but at this point there is much more tangible information to enable final decisions and choices.

Whatever we choose for the project, or whatever gets chosen by others, the main things that need to be done are to

- retain and utilise the design that has evolved and developed during the previous steps of the process;
- make sure that the technical choices support target deliverables of the website and the needs of the target audience; and
- make technical choices that fit with the available skills and resources, that follow good practice, and take advantage of emerging technology.

There are no set standards for which type of machine, which browser, which browser version, which screen size and resolution, and what type of Internet connection (e.g., modem or a broadband variation) the users of our website will be utilising. However, we might be able to anticipate that our website users will mainly be from particular communities, interest groups, socio-economic groups, etc., in which case it is possible to form a view on the typical level (or range) of technology to which those users will have access. Where possible, therefore, we should try to identify any technical specifications that apply to any known or main target groups or individuals and make sure that our implementation is suited, where possible, for those specifications.

This step is placed at this point because there is a good understanding of the scope and depth of the website required and the decisions are needed prior to detailed design work. However, some of the more 'strategic' decisions on technology choices will have been made, or considered, in earlier stages of the project (see Chapter 2), as there is a lead time in acquiring and setting into place new technology environments.

We could implement the same design, or at least one very similar in essence, in quite a variety of technologically based ways. Options include the use of Flash (or equivalent software), Director, Java, embedded media, JavaScript, animated GIF images, etc. The technology selected has a bearing on what can be presented (and how it can be presented) and what can be successfully received and experienced by the user. The following points indicate the scope and complexity of the situation.

The use of software such as Flash and Director (to create animations and visual/audio 'movies') relies on the audience having the appropriate players and plug-ins to handle the media items placed in a webpage. For example, if a movie is created in the latest version of the 'producing' software and the user of the website has an out-of-date player/plug-in, then it is unlikely that the media content will be seen, with the added problem of user confusion and 'alienation'. Software download links on the implemented website are one way to alleviate the problem but can be cumbersome to the user.

A site can be developed with a particular resolution and screen size in mind, but then the user of the website may have different display settings applied or preferred on their machine (e.g., screen resolution of 800×600 or 1024×768 pixels) and/or has a 15″ monitor in front of them instead of the 17″ or 19″ screen possibly used by the developers. This can have drastic impacts on the webpage layout, appreciation of the aesthetic, and understanding of the material. Decisions need to be made regarding designing for all situations or alternatively choosing a particular combination of attributes and about how to inform users about optimum setups where needed.

With streaming audio/video, things are not quite so brittle as they used to be (as several players – e.g., Windows Media, QuickTime, RealMedia – will now play a variety of compression formats), but if the user has no media player software at all or software that does not match the version of the production software, there could be problems. To embed streaming audio/video, the user's browser needs the appropriate plug-in installed, which cannot be relied upon. Browser software installation tends to automate the setup of the plug-ins, but the browser version (and hence the associated plug-ins) could now be old and have out-of-date plug-ins. Relevant software download links on the implementation website should be considered. For 'live' webcasts, audio/video pre-event communication/notification of instructions for users is essential to allow time to set up and test delivery of streamed material.

Loading and interactivity response times are significantly affected by the Internet connection type (e.g., modem or broadband, and level of broadband). The quality of the user experience can be substantially reduced if the timings are slow or very slow for page loading, media playing, etc. PC, Mac, and other environments have (often subtle but significant) differences in how they handle the user interface and also in the availability of software (and software versions) for running on the computers. Our design ideas might rely on special interfaces (e.g., touch screen), but will their presence and use be reasonable to expect?

These are but a few examples, but hopefully they make the point that we must try to identify our main targeted audience and how any prevailing technical constraints or characteristics have to be carefully taken into account in our development. Quite rightly, the issues and information realised by this investigation should affect our choices of multimedia technology (formats and production software), the amount of file compression we employ, file sizes used, screen resolutions/sizes accommodated by our layout designs, media presentation attributes, etc. All of this has to be balanced against the desires for the site in terms of style, content, and presentation.

A further significant factor to be considered is the situation regarding available resources and skills. Most software packages have steep learning curves, and so a decision to choose software in which one has no or minimal skills would only be made if there is no easier alternative and/or there are special reasons to work with that software (to offset the extra learning time and effort involved). The cost of purchasing software licenses is an important aspect, too. To follow or not to follow trends in how current websites are developed and presented is also an issue. The ideal is to try and balance expectations in the marketplace, innovativeness/originality, and appropriateness for the website topic with the available budget, resources, and time.

However, take note that all of the design material produced in this and all other process steps has a construction and presentation that is independent of the technical details of how we code and build. It will be rare that the design details will need to be changed due to technical issues in conceptual or substantive terms. Check back through the documentation of your website design for any specific mention of aspects directly referencing software or other expected technology presence or use. Look at the completed documentation such as the 'web design requirements' list, Review & Reflect report(s), and the purpose, usability, and aesthetic design tables. The combination of these items of documentation will help, at least as a start. It often is the case, however, that the technical aspects have not been too prominent in discussions and analysis so far. There could be so little information already gathered that there is a need to get talking with other members of the project team (including the client representatives) and to do some research and analysis work to uncover new information about audience expectations and needs and about conceptual style preferences of the website owners. The currently available software and hardware options and the available budget will also influence decisions.

Here is a form that will help guide us to build up a comprehensive picture of the situation (Fig. 7.1: Technical considerations). Deciding on technical solutions is crucial to the quest of implementing an effective website, and careful well-founded thought is needed to avoid using technology that is inappropriate. The project team needs to ascertain as solid a case as possible for all the choices and to ensure that all possible problems of technical conflicts and restrictions have been resolved and optimisation realised.

Website Aspect	Technical Selection (i.e., website designed for/with this technology)
PC/Mac/other	All types
Screen size(s)	17″/15″
Screen resolution(s)	800×600
Development software	Dreamweaver
Browsers and versions	Explorer 5+ / Netscape 4.8+
Internet connection	Modem +
Audio formats	RealMedia (some streaming)
Video formats	RealMedia/Flash (some streaming)
Images/animation	gif/jpg
Development/production environments + anomalies	Windows XP (PC) No known anomalies
Backup and recovery/ archiving /version control	Summary: Development – backups to rewritable CD every day. Individual developer so version control is a simple use of saving files under new names when major stages are reached in the development (V1/V2, etc.). After implementation, backups to hard disc and CD each week for first six weeks, then every month. Additional backups made if a major change made to website at any time. The implemented website to be checked every 3 days for any signs of intervention/damage.
	Technical Considerations **Website ID:** World Religions **Date**: Week 6

Fig. 7.1: Technical considerations

For each website aspect, specify the associated technical specification details, collectively defining the technology levels and constraints for the whole website. Take a look at the last two website aspects that need some decision making. It can sometimes happen that websites and website projects look great until the actual implementation. This can be due to becoming aware of certain peculiar characteristics of the webserver system itself (that will host the website) at a very late stage. To be conversant with any anomalies at the early stage of this current step means that procedures can be set in place to avoid implementation difficulties. A simple example is that the PC Windows environment tends to allow long filenames and special characters in those filenames but UNIX webservers do not so readily work with those features. So, for example, to adopt file-naming systems in development that will be compatible with the production environment avoids a great deal of difficulties and delays later.

Critical decisions also are needed in the sphere of backup and recovery/archiving and version control. Any computer system can fail, and that can happen at any time. Recent years have brought the increasing risk of damage and intervention due to hacking and viruses. The nature of the website, the owner, and the audience will contribute to how punishing it would be to lose the presence of the website (and/or data utilised by the website). A backup recovery system is needed to protect the implemented website against losses and reduce downtimes. A system also needs to be put in place during the development cycle of the project.

The exact approach to keeping backups and maintaining version control will depend on in-house rules for these activities – especially if you are working as part of an established development team or if the website is for a medium to large organisation. However, typical characteristics of a suitable system are as follows:

- Backups/recovery/archiving – Keep regular backups of the developing and complete website and any associated data in two or more storage areas (one of a hard-disc variety and one on CD/DVD). This is a minimum – more copies definitely should be kept if the website is of very high value. The frequency of backing up the data used/created by the site will vary according to each situation. The procedure must also adhere to current data-protection legislation relating to the storage of personal data. In addition to backing up files, we need to plan how we will actually 'recover' from a problematic situation – i.e., the procedure in pragmatic terms to exchange corrupt, damaged, or incorrect files with the preferred ones (the latest known intact/correct files). Previous versions of the files can be kept for possible future use by 'archiving' – i.e., storing copies of the files as the design/implementation progresses at various points in its development, and then at appropriate intervals after implementation. The cost of disc space ('permanent' and removable) is so low nowadays that there should be no financial constraints. However, it does take some time and care to effectively manage the process and the materials. Labelling and documenting is important, and this needs to be thought out and agreed on early in the project.

- Version control – This partly relates to being able to trace through the path that the website follows through its development life cycle, but it also is important if several developers are working on the same project. Each team member needs to know which is the latest version of the website, and its component files, and if anyone is currently working on any of the files. File naming can incorporate a naming convention design to help alleviate this potential problem – e.g., adding V1, V2, etc., as a suffix to filenames ('V' refers to 'version'). This is crucial in order to avoid confusion and mistaken use of incorrect versions of files. A typical approach is to make sure that files are 'locked' out from being edited (read only) if someone else is working on the file already. It is also worthwhile to have a clear delineation of responsibility for work done on particular parts of the website to cut down on the number of times that more than one person would need to work on a particular file.

The table (Fig. 7.1) has space for a *summary* of the backup and recovery plans. *Detailed* descriptions of procedures are expected to be written up as a separate report and kept as an active reference document.

Decisions also need to be made regarding the software and hardware development environment for the website project. This topic is discussed in detail in Chapter 9 (software tools), which covers issues such as deciding on technologies to use and indicates the scope of what is available and possible. In essence, websites are typically coded using text editors, or with software that generates the code automatically from options taken via a visual/menu-driven interface, or as a media presentation (e.g., using Flash). A broad range of software is available for creating and manipulating digital images audio, and video for use in or via a website. Some packages have sleep learning curves so purchases and training must be put in place in time for when they are needed.

Exercises

Seminar Topics

1. To what extent should *developer* preference and experience 'drive' the selection of technical options?
2. "Don't use bleeding edge technology" is often-used advice for website developers. Discuss the meaning of the advice and its relevance to modern advances in Internet technology.
3. Discuss the possibilities and any issues re developing a website for a very specific (user) hardware setup.

Tutorial Exercises

1. Give three examples of technical issues that need to be taken into consideration in this step.
2. At what point (in a project) should decisions on technical selection/options be made?
3. What characteristics need to be built into a good backup and version control plan for a typical website design project?

Case Study

1. Make a list of technical issues that specifically need to be considered and resolved in your website project.
2. Complete Fig. 7.1 (Technical Considerations) for your website project. Make brief notes on the main reasoning for those decisions/choices.
3. Construct a detailed plan for backup/recovery and for version control for your website, maximising rigour but minimising any impacts on development time and practice.

7.2 Step 8: Navigation Design, Screen Layouts, Webpage Dialogues, Purpose Mapping, and Content Index

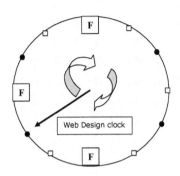

The outcomes of this step form the blueprint of the physical infrastructure of a website. It is where we begin to actually sketch out the detailed visual, structural, and operational design of the website, heavily based on the outcomes of Steps 3–6 but also taking into account any decisions made in other steps. It is where we pave the way for our website to achieve the ambitions set out in the purpose aspirations table, the usability planning table, and the aesthetic planning table, placing key design ideas into the context of the cohesive overall design. This is the last stage of design before commencing the coding, building, and testing phases of the project.

Navigation Design

Although the details of how we design the appearance of the website navigation (e.g., visual clues/links/metaphors) have endless possibilities, there are only two general types of website navigation structure:

- 'Centralised' – All main pages link to each other and all or most pages have the same list of possible links. Some pages might have a few extra and unique links. This may involve the use of frames (with a consistently positioned frame for the links index) or more simply be pages that each have a particular part of the page set aside for the navigation links.
- 'Scattered' – Pages have their own mixture of links, some of which might appear on other pages, but no set pattern. Frames might be involved but are less likely for this navigation type.

The navigation links can be simple text, images, and/or shapes, as part of HTML syntax and possibly using JavaScript, or they could be objects created by such packages as Flash and could be animated.

To an extent, the choice will depend on the overall nature and style of the site. For example, a 'scattered' approach lends itself to more fluidity and flexibility in site structure and user experience. A 'centralised' approach helps to provide consistency and a more controlled, but dependable, experience moving around the site. Some sites have a mixture of the two types of navigation, but usually one type predominates. The choice between the two types should be based on the most suitable style for the website – i.e., in many cases, avoid taking a scattered approach, as it can be confusing to the user and give the impression of poor planning and design. Conversely, the scattered approach can provide more spontaneity and flexibility.

The choice of content for the navigation links (e.g., text, images, interactive menu, etc.) might be influenced by technical preferences and expertise – for example, the programmer might not be comfortable or experienced in constructing and using frames or scripting techniques. However, there is a great deal of help with this aspect when using DHTML-generating software and also from resource websites. Try to be rigorous with how you make your choices – the short-term cost of gaining the necessary skills is always going to be much less than the long-term cost of a design that is inappropriate or inadequate. For much of the design work, the appearance, positioning, operation, overall style, and interaction can be specified in the design without detailing the technicalities of implementation coding – in fact this usually makes for a much stronger and more flexible design.

Usually, we need to try and design the navigation system so that the user of the website can easily recognise 'where they are' in the website and easily be able to recognise how they can move to wherever they wish to go in the site. The style of the navigation system (appearance and actions) needs to be relevant to the purpose, usability, and aesthetic needs and hopes of the site. Study the documentation from previous steps you have completed to form the foundation for the navigation style.

A key factor in deciding on the approach to navigation in a website design is the desired usability characteristics. You will have gone through analysis and decision making in earlier steps to be able to specify the aesthetic and usability planning tables, which provide useful input to the navigation design. Clearly the style and appearance of the navigation should reflect the desired aesthetic and usability characteristics already planned.

The time taken for preparing the interface items for the navigation can be quite significant, as it could involve the creation of special graphical or image objects and possibly creating interactive aspects (e.g., changing the appearance of objects due to mouse action). Also, multimedia objects such as sound and video might need to be prepared to form part of the navigation design.

Some general tips for navigation design are:

- Where appropriate, make the links to other pages/items noticeable and recognisable, and possibly group them together in special areas on the screen (menu areas). 'Curved usability' (see Chapter 3) websites might demand something less clear, though, exploring more abstract and unusual ground.
- Use an appropriate style for the link items, and show care and inventiveness in their creation.
- Consider visual clues to explain/indicate the position of the current page in the whole sitemap structure (e.g., a technique commonly known as 'breadcrumbs'.
- Graphics/images tend to work better and show 'careful' and imaginative design compared with simply using text links.
- Javascript code (widely available as download examples on the Web if needed) can make quite impressive interactive menus or transitions, for example. Some packages (such as Dreamweaver) automate the construction of JavaScript interactivity.
- Multimedia packages such as Flash and equivalents can be used to create navigation schemes that are in effect mini software applications that run on the webpage. They require the user of the website to have the 'player' software (and the appropriate version) for those packages or else the navigation may not be seen unless and until downloads are completed (i.e., if the user doesn't already have the software on their computer).

Let's take a look at the template charts that can be used to document the navigation design structure (i.e., the sitemap) in Figs. 7.2, 7.3, and 7.4 (incidentally, the visual and interactive aspects of the navigation design are dealt with later in this chapter within the screen layout and webpage dialogue sections). For a given website, only one sitemap is needed, but it could be a hybrid of the given template styles. In the rare cases where the site needs to switch between frames and nonframes environments, a hybrid version of the templates would be needed. The term 'frames' refers to where webpages are split into two or more areas on the screen, with each rectangular area having content described by a separate HTML file. The advantage is that it means only part of the screen is replaced by new material when links are selected (which gives slightly speedier loading, streamlines coding of pages, and gives more consistency in screen appearance).

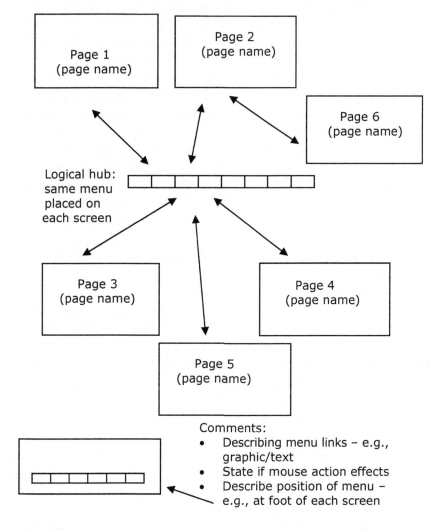

Fig. 7.2: Navigation structure – sitemap (centralised, nonframes)

Let's look at some examples – first the 'centralised' type of navigation – with and without frames in the implementation. Template 1 (Fig. 7.2: Sitemap (centralised, nonframes)) shows an example sitemap having a centralised navigation structure for a nonframe website. It uses the notion of a 'logical hub'. All pages drawn to connect and join at this single 'logical' point can be considered as being able to link to every other page also connecting at this hub. Typically, the 'hub' is a navigation menu that appears on every page, usually in the same screen position.

Any pages that have extra links that are not present on the common navigation menu are shown as direct connections between pages. Figure 7.2 shows an example situation where page 2 links to page 6 but no other pages link to page 6.

Each page should be labelled with as much information as is known at the time of drawing the chart, but also keep the information concise so that the chart is visually clear. In the chart, names should be given to pages or descriptions provided. A centralised navigation structure usually involves the use of a list of links placed close to each other on the page (a navigation menu) and usually in the same position on each page. The position can be noted on the sitemap diagram (the position stated in the template is an example), and if it is known whether graphics/images/text are to be used for the, links, then include an explanatory comment. A comments section for the chart is useful to explain any aspects of the navigation that might not be directly clear from the diagram. The comments section is where you can place any information that further clarifies or defines the navigation design.

The documentation used in this book is designed to help with the design process and decisions in addition to providing documentary evidence of the agreed design. The drawing of the sitemap chart can result in the realisation of something that might not otherwise happen until too late – i.e., the visualisation of the structure can bring ideas together into a cohesive design and also reveal any problematic aspects that previously have not been noticed. For example, to see a 'spider's web' of pages linked together in a complex and confusing manner raises the question of whether that is suitable and absolutely necessary, enabling the opportunity to change and simplify the website structure design before any building and coding takes place. This could mean changes to the scope of the website or the way that aspects are grouped together.

Figure 7.3 is a frames example of a structural navigation design showing how the frames structure can be represented and then labelled to indicate the main purpose of each frame on the screen. The lines

connecting to the various pages are placed to signify the position at which
the pages are displayed on the screen (i.e., which space on the screen is
used as the display area for each subsequently selected page). The
template example shows the frames structure typically found in websites,
but websites can have the screen divided up differently (e.g., with menus
on the right of the screen), so sitemaps need to clearly indicate such
features.

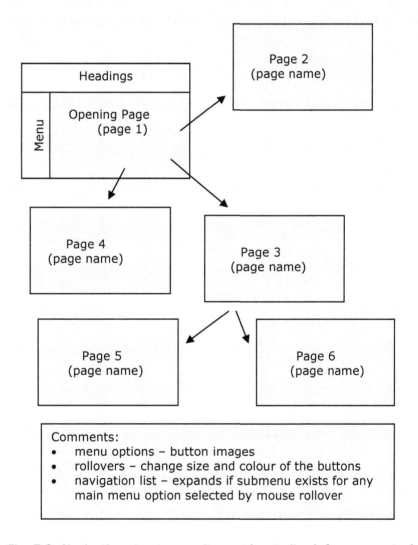

Fig. 7.3: Navigation structure – sitemap (centralised, frames version)

At this stage, it should also be possible to specify details about the navigation area – the structure and appearance plus any interactivity envisaged (e.g., mouse rollovers, etc.). This can be explained in the comments section or perhaps sketched on the diagram.

The boxes representing the pages should be labelled with page names and/or the main purpose or use of that page. Any pages that are exclusively accessed via a particular page and not the navigation bar are represented by line connections to that page (e.g., pages 5 and 6 in the template link from page 3). If any of the pages in the website are displayed full-screen (rather than within a frame), then this information must be visually indicated or stated in the comments section on the chart along with anything else that is important and relevant to the site navigation.

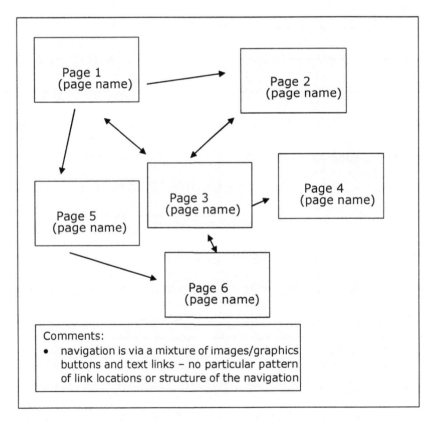

Fig. 7.4: Navigation structure – sitemap (scattered) template

Figure 7.4 (Sitemap (scattered) template) shows how a sitemap can be illustrated for a website having a somewhat irregular navigation design.

Pages tend to have differing sets of links. This 'scattered' structure is sometimes necessary to satisfy the unique needs of a site.

There is no particular pattern followed by the links, and each page has differences in navigation connections. As with the other sitemaps, a comments section is used to explain aspects not covered visually by the diagram itself. The links (although different for each page) could be placed in a recognisable area on each page if that type of consistency is desired.

Figure 7.5 shows our case study example of a navigational structure diagram (a sitemap), in this case a 'centralised, nonframes' type.

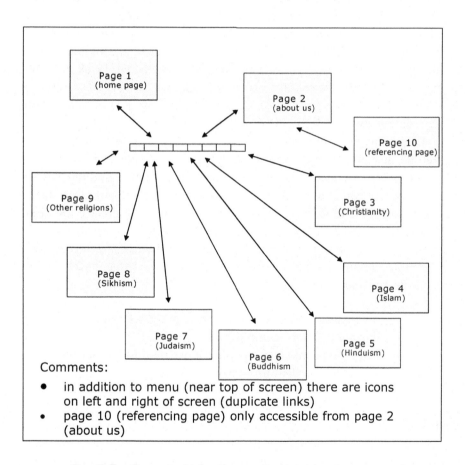

Fig. 7.5: Case study for the navigation structure example

Navigation can typically be via menus, image maps, and/or separate items spread around a page. Menus and 'separate items' can use images, graphics, text, and/or mouse action as a basis for links. Image maps use images (broken up into two or more areas so that cursor position on an image is fundamental in choosing which link is to be taken) for links. The appearance and style of the navigation is often a website feature that is key in impressing (or otherwise) a visitor to the site. Careful and creative use of graphics and interactivity is typically an effective approach. Interactivity can be implemented into the navigation design using JavaScript or Flash, for example. As the years progress, it is less easy to come up with new and original ideas, but the effort to do so pays dividends in the overall design impact. There are many (free) download sites for scripting and tutorials that help with creating innovative navigation designs, and these would typically be used in conjunction with imaging packages such as Adobe Photoshop. Interactive JavaScript code can be automatically created via taking options in DHTML-generating software such as Dreamweaver. Chapter 9 goes into advice and options regarding software selection in more detail.

Originality, identity, and context suitability are very important in website design generally, and this applies most definitely to navigation design – i.e., to creating original visual/sonic elements, finding ways to make the navigation interesting and stylish. When trying out ideas, keep a close eye on the usability and aesthetic characteristics already identified as being appropriate and necessary for your website.

As part of fulfilling target usability and aesthetic characteristics, the navigation design should offer an appropriate 'knowledge' to the user of, typically, the following:

- awareness of the scope and nature of the website;
- current position within the site;
- action to be taken to complete a desired task at that page or to locate another feature or part of the site.

The 'appropriateness' of the extent, clarity, and style of delivery of that 'knowledge' depends on the identified usability (broadly speaking, the degree of usability straightness or curvedness desired) and aesthetic characteristics. The details of these ambitions will have been specified in the usability planning table and the aesthetic planning table (Step 5 of the process).

Consider the use of the following aspects and items to help achieve these attributes:

- logos and graphics that distinguish the community, activity, company, organisation, or whatever is served or represented by the website;
- images or other items that draw attention as navigation aids to the context or functionality offered;
- sound (background or those triggered by action or movement) designed to help form associations with structure and location;
- menus and lists, page names and numbers, cascading titles, all ways of indicating position in the total site hierarchy;
- a search facility (text keyword) and/or extended menus to help find the location of exactly what is being sought by the user;
- emotive use of colours, patterns, and soundscapes;
- strategies to creatively provide obscurity and adventure for example (if relevant) as an alternative to clarity and swiftness.

The chosen intentions for the navigation design style have to be written out and can be sketched out in advance of working on overall screen layouts.

During this current stage, it is useful to work with a summary checklist to confirm whether the navigation design upholds and supports ideas previously decided and/or if there are any new points to carry forward to subsequent steps of the design process. The following table (Table 7.1: Navigation design checklist), which shows example information from our case study, might help.

A simple 'yes' or 'no' is needed in the 'Satisfied' column. The 'Comments/Actions' column is where we write something to briefly note any new design ideas introduced into the navigation design at this stage and/or aspects that need some further thought and action (but sufficiently satisfied to continue on with the design process).

Incidentally, increasingly webpages are formed in Flash or similar new media software packages rather than completely in HTML/DHTML. The navigation design work, however, as with all other aspects of following the process described in this book, is independent of the implementation software environment.

Table 7.1: Navigation design checklist

Item to Check Against	Satisfied?	Comments/Actions
Web design requirements list	Yes	check 'rolling' aspect of menu. Clear?
Purpose aspirations table	Yes	
Usability planning table	Yes	Consider use of icons/ graphics on navigational menu(s)
Aesthetic planning table	Yes	
Review and Reflect (1) report	Yes	
General points: In testing, reflect on whether the use of the two navigational aspects works ok. Confusing? Does the scrolling of menu items look ok? Check speed. Are the pages too busy (menus obscured?)?		
Navigation Design Checklist **Website ID:** **Date:**	World Religions Weeks 4/5	

Hence all aspects of the design work can be applied to whatever software environment is used for the implementation of the website. The nature of the desired navigation design might, though, influence the choice of implementation environment, along with the characteristics of available skills and software resources.

Now that the structure of the navigation design has been defined and the style considered, the details of appearance and mechanisms are specified within 'screen layouts' and 'webpage dialogue designs'.

Screen Layouts

We are now at quite a strong point in the early stages of a web design project. We have a clear view on purpose, usability, and aesthetic needs for our website – all of which are nicely supporting our overall aspirations and vision for the website. We also now have specified the spinal chord for our website – the structure and main style of our navigation system. Now it is time to begin 'fleshing out' our ideas by designing the layouts, interactivity, and processing for all of our pages.

Let's begin this next phase by designing the layouts for each of the envisaged webpages. Figure 7.6 shows a screen layout design template. It shows the shape of the screen with designated areas for aspects as they will appear on the webpage. The exact size, shape, and position of each component on the page will depend on the specific needs of each page. An example layout can be seen in Fig. 7.7, based on our case study.

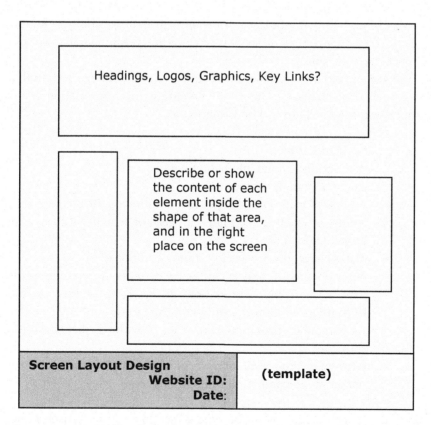

Fig. 7.6: Screen layout design template

Use the main design information you have already derived (in particular, the website design requirements list, the purpose aspirations table, the usability planning table, the aesthetics planning table, and the navigation design) to guide you in what is needed for your screen layout concept. For example, it might be the case that the targeted aesthetics suggest having a varying screen design format that creates humour or evokes serenity or another emotion. It is for this reason that considerable thought is needed in designing the first screen design for the site, one that might be used as a template for the rest of the pages. Usually, the first page designed is the opening page of the site, the main/home page.

The screen layout template (Fig. 7.6) shows the screen area split into several sections. It shows the visual structure of the webpage and how the whole screen can be broken up into regions that hold various types of content and media types – text, graphics, images, multimedia items/ controls, etc. It helps to label each area to describe the purpose or type of content that will appear in those spaces. The drawn spaces don't need to be exact (although that would be of benefit if the dimensions are known already) but do need to reasonably reflect the positions, shapes, and proportions expected.

The screen layout design diagram could have a comments section that gives further information to help understanding and appreciation of the layout design and include such information as

- navigation style;
- description of main interaction details;
- any animation included;
- sources of material – images, text, multimedia items (including a note on whether the material exists or whether it has yet to be created/edited);
- if any items only appear in certain conditions;
- notes on special 'player' software, or other software, that the user of that page would need in order to access material fully (this can inform additions to the design in some cases – for example, providing links to download player/plug-in software);
- page-load time estimations, plus comments on ideas for image/sound compression, streaming, etc.

An actual screen print of a prototype screen layout is also useful (Fig. 7.7) but should be in addition to a drawn screen design layout.

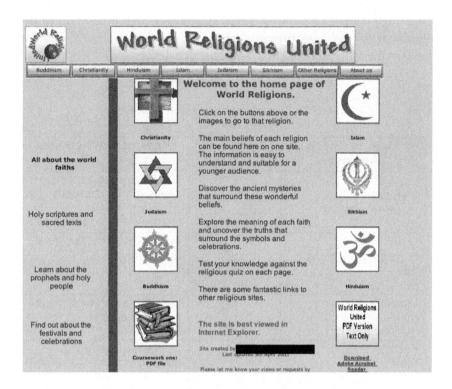

Fig. 7.7: Screen print of 'World Religions' homepage

A screen layout design has to be completed for each page of the website, and several drafts might be needed to arrive at a design that fully satisfies all purpose, usability, and aesthetic requirements. However, where pages are able to follow the same pattern, designs can be re-used. To see the layout of each page emerge is to gradually see the whole website design unfold. Meetings with user representatives are a crucial element at this stage to get feedback and input on these prototype designs.

Use a checklist (see Table 7.2: 'Screen layout design checklist') to keep track of whether existing ideas for your website design are supported by your detailed screen layout designs. A general point: the more closely each subsequent design task matches the desires and expectations of all previous steps in the design process, the more likely that the final design will be appropriate and effective – and this applies of course to this current task of designing the screen layouts. So the checklist needs to include all design documentation items that are outcomes of previous steps in the process. A checklist should be completed for each separate screen layout and/or for a set of screen layouts. It takes time to do all this, together with close attention to a large volume of detail, but the reward comes in the form of robust and very effective designs.

Table 7.2: Screen layout design checklist

Item to Check Against	Satisfied?	Comments/Actions
Web design requirements list	No	Low/high spec aspect needs more attention
Purpose aspirations table	OK	Include 'search' facility if time allows
Usability planning table	OK	Location awareness could be made clearer
Aesthetic planning table	OK	Is site 'welcoming' enough?
Review and Reflect (1) report	OK	Get feedback (users) on colours chosen
Navigation design	OK	
General points: None		
Screen Layout Design Checklist **Website ID:** **Date:**	World Religions Weeks 6/7	

'OK' and 'No' are terms that can be used in the 'satisfied' column, with comments and actions stated where needed. Any problems are to be resolved either within this step or perhaps via the next 'Review and Reflect' step (Step 9).

Webpage Dialogues

As part of the screen layout design, some information about interactions and interactivity has been included that relates to each of the pages in the envisaged website.

Now it is time to specify this in much more detail with 'webpage dialogues'. For each page, we need to decide how the user will be able to interact with the webpages and illustrate the nature of those interactions in the documentation (see Figure 7.8: Webpage dialogue template).

The template shows how each interaction between the user and the webpage can be described, so that collectively we can observe the complete potential dialogue. The aim is to utilise as much visualisation of the dialogue as possible and use text to support understanding. Each interaction should be included, using one row of the three columns to describe each interaction, giving details of 'item action' (the action made by the user with or on the webpage item in question – visual style), 'reaction' (a text description of the webpage response to that action), and 'consequence' (the resulting situation arising on the webpage due to the action and response – visual style).

Figure 7.8 shows a few typical examples of interactions and how the three columns can be used to describe those interactions. The examples indicate how user actions (e.g., mouse-over, mouse click, etc.,) can be represented visually. The precise way in which you illustrate actions, items, screen positions, etc., is flexible (you could adopt the represented ideas in our examples and/or develop an in-house style). One important aspect is to design the diagrammatic aspects of the dialogue sheet to indicate all the details that are known at that stage – e.g., positions of interactive items on the page, names of images/objects, etc. The important thing is to use clear visualisation together with concise labelling and descriptions and that as a project team you use a consistent set of standards for the dialogue documentation so that it is quick and easy for you and others to observe and understand that documentation. To help people understand the documentation, it is a good idea to provide a 'key' for the diagrams utilised. In cases where the dialogues need some supporting explanations, include a comments section in the chart.

Dialogues are needed for each of the pages in your project website – possibly beginning with the main opening page of the website and following each subsequent webpage in turn. This can follow a sequence of links from that first main page or some other order that suits the project.

There is no strict order in which interactions for a particular page should be covered in the sheet (or sheets, if there are a lot of interactions for a particular webpage), but you might find it useful to go methodically from left to right and from top to bottom of the webpage. Other ways are to place the interactions in order of 'importance' (which might in fact be difficult to decide) or perhaps in the order in which you envisage a user operating the page.

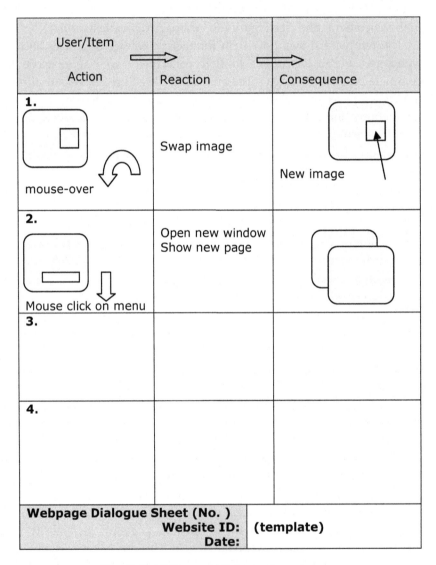

Fig. 7.8: Web page dialogue template

The complete set of webpage dialogues should collectively and individually correspond to the purpose targets envisaged for the website (see Step 4), reflect usability and aesthetic requirements as specified in Step 5, and match navigation design aspects designed earlier. The combination of the screen layouts and the webpage dialogues should match the total hopes and aspirations for the website. The completeness of this combination of design elements is further tested by constructing 'purpose maps' later in this chapter.

It is quite likely that there will be more than one set of ideas for navigation, screen layouts, and webpage dialogue design. This is not a problem – construct draft layouts for each design idea and perhaps some screen mock-ups, and organise an evaluation session, with representatives of the user and client teams included in the session group.

To finalise this part of the process, it is recommended that a webpage dialogue checklist be completed (Table 7.3). We need to use the checklist be help keep track of the extent to which we feel that the aims for purpose, usability, and aesthetic characteristics have successfully been achieved in the designs. It also helps us consider the extent to which the webpage dialogues collectively adhere to and satisfy the demands and expectations of key components of the detailed design work completed thus far. Each time a formal check (for compatibility and consistency) is made between design components, and between design needs/ideas, the greater the chance of making an effective, appropriate, and coherent implementation.

The extent to which this checklist task proves to be simple and straightforward will largely be a measure of how much careful attention has been given previously to the specification of each component being checked. All the components emanate from the same original core requirements and desires (ascertained from the continued communications between developers and users/clients – and the analysis of the information gleaned), and so cohesiveness should follow naturally. The design outcomes from each step are used as a basis for working on the subsequent step's design. The checklist approach (which is used several times in the design process described in this book) is a very visible way of making judgments on completeness and consistency and of identifying any problems. Any difficulties or gaps must be addressed now or in the later Review and Reflect step (Step 9). Some aspirations and expectations might have to be respecified (or removed or postponed) if too costly (in time and effort) or difficult to implement.

The third column is used to give comments and to describe actions suggested to rectify any difficulty or shortfall. In fact, even if an item has

Table 7.3: Webpage dialogue design checklist

Item to Check Against	Satisfied?	Comments/Actions
Web design requirements list	OK	
Purpose aspirations table	OK	n.b. consider using a 'search' facility
Usability planning table	OK	
Aesthetic planning table	OK	Be careful to avoid clutter – might need attention
Review and Reflect (1) report	OK	
Navigation design	OK	
Screen layout designs	OK	
General points: None		
Webpage Dialogue Design Checklist **Website ID:** **Date:**	World Religions Week 7	

been deemed to be 'ok', there might be some comments that need to be made to help any future reviews perhaps or to draw attention to any important issues or thoughts that are emerging.

Purpose Mapping

A purpose map is a device to describe how a user would, in pragmatic terms, use the website to achieve each and every specific purpose of the website. For example, if one purpose was to 'listen to an audio track', then the purpose mapping would need to indicate how the user would achieve that target purpose. The action and route needed would be described – with as much visualisation as possible – e.g., using icons rather than long text descriptions. The task of drawing out the purpose maps also has the advantage that designers are able to check if each specific target purpose is satisfied by particular design elements and that the series of user actions for each purpose is reasonable and efficient. Figure 7.9 shows an example of a purpose map and acts as a template.

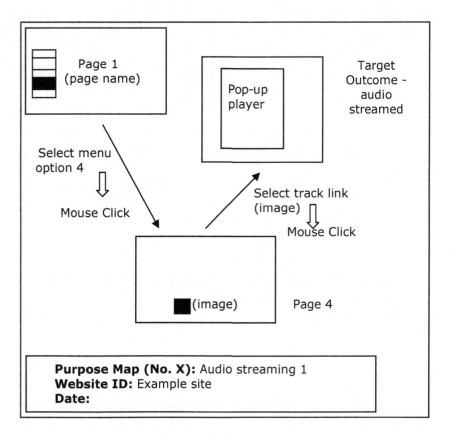

Fig. 7.9: Purpose mapping

The main reference sources to ascertain the list of purposes to map are the purpose aspirations table, the screen layouts, and the webpage dialogue sheets. Each target purpose must be covered by at least one purpose map (some outcomes can be realised in more than one way/route). The screen layout and webpage dialogues perhaps will help most in identifying the process route for users to achieve each target purpose.

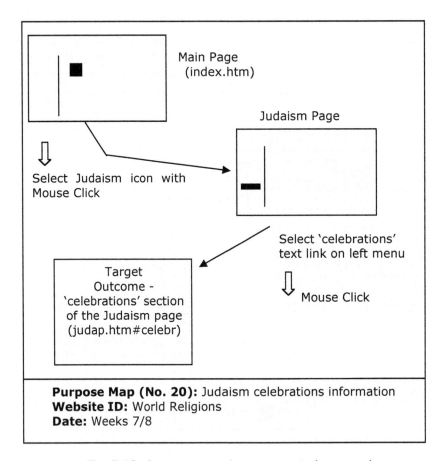

Fig. 7.10: Purpose mapping – case study example

Each of these target purposes has to be broken down into discrete steps that the user should take to access and/or operate/experience the item in question. Figure 7.10 shows an example purpose map from our case study. Please note that some purposes can be achieved simply by observing a page (i.e., without any special key presses or other interactions).

The purpose mapping documentation can be used later as part of user documentation, but at this stage it is a good way for the designer to establish clearly and methodically how the proposed design enables each target purpose to be achieved. The process of building up the purpose maps might draw attention to usability problems (or simply that a target purpose is missing or incomplete), in which case possible changes to the design should be noted. The changes could be made immediately or considered fully later in Step 9 (Review and Reflect).

Content Index

The content index is a listing of exactly what material is to be contained in the website, on/via which particular webpages, from which source(s), and any processing or preparation needed for the sourced material prior to implementation. It also notes the extent to which the information will need to be updated during the life of the website. Table 7.4 ('Content index') shows an example of how this information can be documented. The index is best organised to list items for each page and could be divided into topic areas.

Table 7.4: Content index

Item	Media Type/ Format	Source	Processing/ Preparation	Static/ Dynamic	Date and % Readiness
banner	wrul.jpg (image)	new	Photoshop	static	Week 4– ready
Content Index **Website name:** World Religions **Webpage name:** Main page (index.htm) **Date:** Weeks 7/8					

This documentation gives you the opportunity to identify any possible problems in obtaining or preparing items and allows checking for completeness during material acquisition. Although the index has to be completed at this point, the actual acquisition and preparation of material would normally be in parallel alongside other process steps. The '% Readiness' information should be updated if and when key progress is made regarding an item, including the date when the point is reached. In the 'Processing/Preparation' column, there could be a note of who has been allocated the task. 'Static/Dynamic refers to whether item is expected to change/evolve.

Exercises

Seminar Topics

1. Discuss why it is suggested to design the navigation scheme before screen layouts and dialogues. Would it matter too much if the aspects were completed in a different order?
2. Analyse the extent to which it is felt that navigation design style should be governed by tradition/trends in the market-place or be innovatively personalised for each specific website.
3. Discuss the extent to which it is possible to *know* if our webpage dialogue design is likely to *work* and be *appropriate.*

Tutorial Exercises

1. What might you typically place in the 'comments section' of your navigation structure design sheet?
2. For a particular website, which webpage would be a good choice for the first screen layout design sheet? What are the criteria for selection?
3. What items of documentation should you include in your checklists for your purpose maps and your webpage dialogue designs?

Case Study

1. Think about your project website. Write bullet points to summarise the main information that will help you design your navigation, screen layouts, and dialogues (use your knowledge from previous steps of the process as a basis).
2. Construct the various sheets and tables necessary for you to complete and record navigation design, screen layout designs, webpage dialogue designs, the purpose mapping, and the content index for your project website.
3. Study the checklist tables for this process step to consider if any comments and/or actions, and decide if action is required immediately or if items needing action can wait until the next step is under way (Step 9 - Review and Reflect).

7.3 Step 9: Review and Reflect (2)

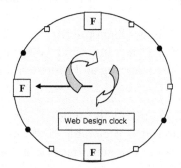

The 'web design' time has reached 9 o'clock – we are now into the latter stages of the design and implementation process cycle.

To review and reflect on any project is a vital ingredient to success – reviewing progress, decisions, and plans and reflecting on requirements, possibilities, and constraints. Are we on schedule for the targeted deliverables? What issues and problems need attention? And so on.

Each of the three Review and Reflect steps (n.b. this is the second of these) has the purpose of studying and evaluating requirements, decisions, and designs and design ideas, plus any related issues that urgently need to be resolved.

The following are typical aspects that should be included for consideration in this particular Review and Reflect step:

- understanding of the specified design needs;
- how well the detailed design matches the design requirements identified during the project;
- project plan – the meeting of deadlines and costs, and any unresolved problems;
- recognition of successes and any knowledge dissemination needs across the team, and any resourcing issues;
- user–developer communication and integration issues;
- any decisions or information urgently needed and/or proving difficult to resolve or ascertain;
- study of all main design documentation produced to date to find unresolved issues/difficulties and anomalies/conflicts.

This second scheduled 'Review and Reflect' step is as strategically placed as the first one. It marks the end of detailed design and is immediately prior to the beginning of the actual coding and building of the website – an ideal time to pause a while to make the checks described. Up to this point, we have

- identified the overall ambitions and aspirations of the project;
- made a project plan;

- defined the detailed and specific purpose, usability, and aesthetic needs, plus associated design ideas to satisfy those needs;
- decided on the relevant technical issues and options;
- designed the navigation, screen layouts, and webpage dialogues, and completed purpose mapping and content index documentation.

This formal checking and evaluation phase is needed before continuing with coding and implementation. It is preferable, and likely, that all or most aspects will be resolved within this step, but it might be necessary to reduce or change expectations if the problem is too costly (in time or resources) or difficult to resolve. It might be necessary to return to one of the previous steps to thoroughly go through a process step again (a 'flashback'). Some problems perhaps could be flagged for resolution at a specific later stage.

Step 10 and onwards should not be commenced until everyone is happy with the outcomes and deliverables of this current Review and Reflect step and hence satisfied with everything produced so far in the project. Remember that although it can be painful to notice and then have to address problems, it is much more favourable than missing a problem and having to deal with the consequences later when deep into the coding/implementation stages. Poor or incomplete designs will be revealed at some point and in some way, and if this happens in the latter stages of a project or after implementation, recovery can be very costly in both time and resources.

All of the website design documentation, and hence all of the outcomes of the steps, has to be double-checked and cross-checked for completeness and cohesiveness. The procedure for completing this checking is similar to Review and Reflect (1) and comprises a mixture of

- individual analysis;
- group discussion and analysis;
- team reporting and study of all project design documentation (including previous Review and Reflect reports).

Part of the process in this step is to specify deadlines for any critical aspects that need attention and to allocate tasks to team members. As in all Review & Reflect steps, we use the R&R report template (see Table 7.5, which includes an example reported item) to make it easier for future tracking of findings and actions.

The table helps to organise the content of the Review and Reflect report so that the 'problems' are clearly identified and that the required action is detailed and its completion monitored. The report operates like a 'sign-off' checklist sheet, whereby we build up a list of items that need attention, note what we feel is needed, and record whether and when the item is resolved successfully.

Table 7.5: R&R report

Item	Source	Comments/ Action	Successfully Resolved Date and Solution
1. Menu list – in left column	Navigation design (main page)	Clarify if list is complete and consider using visuals	To be resolved
Website name/ID: Direct input to this report (documentation items):		World Religions Screen layout	
BWD Step: (6, 9, or 12): Date:		2 Week 8	

Exercises

Seminar Topics

1. Do you think it is too late to Review and Reflect at this stage? (Has enough time been spent on checking already?) Discuss.
2. Can you envisage any problems that might result in a project being totally halted/cancelled due to the outcomes of this Review and Reflect step?
3. "I enjoy reviewing and reflecting – it gives me a chance to find problems to solve." Discuss the project positives and negatives related to this viewpoint.

Tutorial Exercises

1   What information, and which sources, are needed as input to this Review and Reflect BWD step?
2. Give three examples of problems or issues that you could imagine finding at this stage.
3. How do we 'track' progress on problematic aspects revealed and reported in this step?

Case Study

1. Gather all the documentation that you have produced so far in your project and check through it all again.
2. Spend time on each aspect according to the level of double-checking you feel is needed.
3. Reflect on all the previously created design documentation you have studied, and note any relevant comments or actions required (on the R&R (2) report form).
4. Decide whether the project is at a point where you can continue immediately with Step 10 or if work is needed prior to that.

CHAPTER EIGHT

Creating the Website

Overview

This chapter deals with the final implementation stages of a website design project – coding, building, testing, and evaluating the completed website. The design documentation, which has been carefully constructed during the project, is used as a blueprint to create the website and later to assess its effectiveness and appropriateness.

This chapter addresses the implementation process, not programming techniques or software skills. It does not deal with instructions on how to code the syntax of HTML (Hyper Text Markup Language) or DHTML, nor detailed instructions on how to use software that generates DHTML (e.g., Dreamweaver) or creates new media content, although you will find useful resource information on the material on the book's website.

Section 3 deals with selecting implementation software and with issues related to managing the hosting and running of a website on the Internet.

Give and Gain

If you give time to this chapter (let's say 50 minutes or so, plus time for the exercises), this is what you will gain:

- guidance in the process of completing one of the final stages of a website project – the construction of the website itself;
- a comprehensive view of what is needed to turn the detailed design material into a working website;
- an understanding of how to test and evaluate your website.

8.1 Step 10: Coding and Building

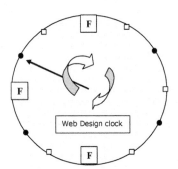

In Step 7, a series of technical decisions had to be made concerning the software and hardware environments to be used and targeted for developing and implementing the website code. The detail of this current step will partially depend on those decisions – e.g., whether you are planning to use a text editor or a GUI-based DHTML code generator, and if target users are expected to be Apple MAC-based, have broadband, etc. There were several aspects considered in Step 7, and the outcomes of those deliberations should be studied again now so that the technology, environments, and approaches used in the coding and building are the most suitable.

Technical support personnel are likely to be needed to set up the hardware and software, especially if it is a first project and if the setup is new. We can use the information from decisions in Step 7 to guide how the various elements of the building process will be implemented. This is especially important in team projects, so that consistency of formats and integration is maintained.

In the chapter on the topic of software tools (Chapter 9), we discuss software technology that is typically utilised in building and implementing websites – you might wish to look ahead again at this chapter to refer to the guidelines given. In conjunction with what you gained from working through Step 7 (Technical selections/issues), it could help with selecting particular detailed technical software/hardware options for implementing the designed website. A general rule of thumb, however, is to use techniques with which you are already familiar and/or those about which you have good evidence for their effectiveness – e.g., as seen via other website projects.

For any website, the aspects that need to be constructed or created can be categorised into the following list:

- text content,
- multimedia content – audio, images, video, animation,
- streaming infrastructure for audio/video,
- logo/graphics,
- webpage layout design,
- website structure, navigation, and interactivity design,
- webpage formation.

The mix of multimedia items and formats varies from site to site, as does whether streaming (where audio and video are able to be experienced whilst the media file content is being downloaded from a website) is used.

A typical combination of 'build' tasks and some possible entries for associated software are indicated in Table 8.1 (Task-software list). The example software packages mentioned in Table 8.1 are given as an indicative list and not necessarily as recommendations, although they are in typical use. Not all of the tasks shown in Table 8.1 would be needed for a particular website project, and it is likely that other tasks would need to be added, depending on the exact nature and scope of the site.

It might seem a very daunting task to implement your website – so many pages, so many aspects to create and include. If you are part of a team, then at least there is help at hand and a split of responsibilities. In team and/or individual projects, there is the task of scheduling and co-ordinating all of the work done and making sure everything integrates effectively. Chapter 2 (The World of Website Design) discusses the preparation needed ahead of a website design and implementation project, which might include HTML/DHTML and software tool training (e.g., if this is your first, or one of your first, website design experiences).

There are many online sources for tutorials and textbooks for purchase (please see the book's website for references), and there is also the option of short specialised training courses.

Table 8.1: Task-software list example

Tasks	Software
Overall website (DHTML code) generation	Dreamweaver, Frontpage
Manual coding of DHTML/text	Notepad, Textpad, Simpletext
Still images – edit	Adobe Photoshop, Fireworks
Moving image – edit/produce	Imovie, Premiere, Finalcutpro, QuickTime, RealMedia
Sound – edit/process	Goldwave, Cooledit
Image/sound compression and streaming	RealMedia, Quicktime, Windows Media
Movie / animation / website construction	Flash, Director
Task-Software List **Website ID:**	N/A (general example)
Date:	N/A (general example)

By following the process described in this book, there will be the advantage of having a very detailed and carefully thought-out design for your website and a comprehensive set of documentation that describes and validates that design. This is where all of that hard work leading up to this point pays off – the detailed and documented design forms a clear roadmap for this programming/building phase.

Often, it is a team task to build a website, and so duties for the various aspects, and the numerous items in each category, can be delegated and spread across the team. It is necessary to make a detailed list of items to be produced (for each webpage) and to allocate names and target dates for those items (see Table 8.2 – 'Aspect/items build list'). The previously completed screen layouts and the webpage dialogue documentation are used to ensure all items are included for each page. Sources and/or responsibilities for an item type may vary, and if so, additional rows can be added to the table so that this level of information can be entered (i.e., an item type such as 'text' split into two or more sub-categories of the text items needed).

Table 8.2: Aspect/items build list

Item	ID	Source(s) of Material	Copyright Clearance	Completion and/or Progress Comment	Target Date
Text – topic introductions	FK	Original		Yes – week 7	Week 7
Text – detailed descriptions	FK	Extracts + summaries from Web, book, and/or own ref. material	Needed for some extracts	Be ready to prepare/select new text	Week 7
Images of people, objects, scenes	FK	New pics and ref. material/archive	Needed for some pics	Prepare/select new images	Week 7
Graphics – logos, titles, etc.	FK	Original		S	Week 8
Animations	FK	Original		S	Week 8
Audio, video, streaming setup	FK	Archive recordings	Needed		Week 9
Webpage layout – finalise design	FK	Navigation design, screen layout, webpage dialogues		Yes – week 6	Week 6
Webpage formation	FK	Webpage dialogues		S	Week 8
Page background + transitions	FK	Original/archive		S	Weeks 8/9
Other:					

Aspect/Items Build List

Webpage name (ID):   Main Page
Project name (ID):   World Religions
Sheet No.: / Date: 1 of 1 / Week 7

Where possible, narrow down the responsibility for each item to a single person (and put initials or names in the 'ID' responsibility column). If several people are grouped together to look after a certain aspect, then define who takes overall responsibility and/or split that aspect down so that there is an identifiable person for specific components of the aspect. This simplifies the task of *managing* the 'build' process, helps with version control, and means that each item has personal attention – with the associated responsibility for quality completion.

The source column is to indicate if the items have to be created as original material or if part or all of the item is to be sourced from existing material, which could already be owned by the client/developers or obtained externally. Items that need copyright clearance need to be identified as such and the table updated once clearance approval is obtained or denied. A simple 'tick' plus the date is all that is needed to indicate the completion of an item (in the 'Completion +/or Progress Comment' column). If the item is still 'in-progress', then put a brief comment or an 'S' to indicate it has been started – if left blank, it indicates that work on the task has not yet begun.

The comments are used to help with further work on an item or to draw attention to anything that needs to be recorded to help in subsequent steps. Target dates are useful for managing project task scheduling. At the foot of the table, ID information is added, plus the date and the sheet no. (if more than one sheet is needed for a webpage).

Once it is established that the aspect/build lists are complete and satisfactory, the building phase can commence. The exact order in which the webpages, and aspects within each page, should be completed varies, partly depending on availability of team personnel and opportunities to source the required material. Often, the page intended as the opening page is developed first, followed by a hierarchy of pages that lead from that main (home) page. Each page has to follow a development process that enables completeness to be considered and progress tracked – as shown in Fig. 8.1 (Webpages build cycle).

Figure 8.1 shows that the starting point is to study design documentation previously completed to help in the construction of the aspect/items build list for each webpage (in particular, the purpose aspirations and the usability/aesthetic planning tables, navigation designs, screen layouts, the webpage dialogue sheets, purpose maps, and the content index). Once everything has been checked and the team is happy that everything is included and covered in the 'aspect/items build list', then the various practical tasks of carrying out the work need to be scheduled in detail. In

Step 2 (BWD) of the project, the time and task analysis work will have identified estimated times, durations, and personnel needed for this part of the project. Now it is time to fine-tune those estimates and distributions of work and make them much more detailed and realistic. The project plan needs to take into account experiences so far with the project and all new knowledge about the tasks in hand. All the content items for the website need to be acquired/created and then incorporated into the building of the webpages.

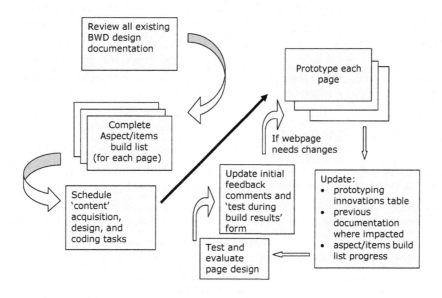

Fig. 8.1: Webpages build cycle

This stage of the process is iterative – a cycle of tasks repeated for each page until it is acceptable (i.e., a protyping approach taken for the actual building and coding of the webpages). The main page for the website (the 'homepage') is probably the best one to build first, as this will form the main portal for users accessing the website. Gather together the component material content for that page and then start building using the 'aspect/items build list' documentation together with all design documentation created earlier in the project.

During this coding and building step, it is expected that there will be some changes and enhancements made to the details of the website design. This is a reflection of how some ideas and problems only reveal themselves when actually constructing and trying out pages and when sourcing/preparing detailed content material. As a team, you need to have an agreed procedure for proposing and approving such changes to the design. The procedure should be swift and 'inclusive' but have sufficient rigour that suggestions are fully considered and all impacts analysed. Above all else, it is imperative that the changes improve the support and achievement of purpose, usability, and/or aesthetic needs. An important feature of the procedure for making and approving the changes is that the whole team is made aware of each change in case they recognise a direct or indirect impact on other areas of the design and implementation that has not yet been noticed.

As part of each prototyping iteration, updates are applied to the project design documentation – summaries being placed in the 'prototyping innovations' table (see Table 8.3), progress updated on the 'aspect/items build list', and changes made to any previous documentation impacted by the latest prototype. Mainly, changes are documented on screen layouts, webpage dialogues, and navigation design sheets, noting the key design changes on the 'prototyping innovations' form. Screenshots of prototype designs can be used instead of redrawing the screen layouts. The number of changes is likely to be few (assuming that work during the preceding design steps has been reasonably meticulous – settling on designs details that are appropriate and comprehensive) but needs to be noted so that the documentation is complete and up-to-date.

The prototype design then needs to be evaluated by testing the response from other team members and/or selected target users of the site. Use the 'initial feedback comments' form to briefly document the findings (Table 8.4). Problems and ideas arising out of these comments need to be indicated on the 'testing during build results form' (Table 8.5) together with ideas identified as resolutions to the problem. This table is discussed more fully later. These resolution ideas then need to be applied to form a new prototype implementation, beginning a new iteration.

Although some changes are triggered by feedback from the testing carried out during this step, the final details of amendments largely result from the pragmatic experiences and enlightened perceptions realised during the process of prototyping the next iteration of the page(s). To an extent, the testing during the prototype iterations pre-empts full testing (Step 11), but by doing evaluation testing now and including target users where possible, it helps to keep things on track for a fully working and satisfactory website. A flow of testing and reacting to the feedback during this current step will make Step 11 much easier and will help avoid the higher costs (in timeliness and person-hours) of making what might be greater changes and corrections later.

Progressively work through the building of all webpages comprising the project website. If it is an individual project, then it usually works best to 'fan out' from the homepage following the link structure indicated in your sitemap documentation. If it is a team project, it is easier and often necessary to work on two or more pages in parallel at any one time. Follow an iterative sequence of developing incremental prototypes of the webpages interspersed with user testing/feedback and documentation updating as described above. Any design documentation affected has to be updated. These updates are necessary so that the project documentation remains coherent and hence keeps its value in terms of its use in website maintenance work and in future projects. In the next steps of the process, in the maintenance of the website later in its life, and in future development projects, a significant benefit is obtained from the accurate and comprehensive documentation of the changes.

When carrying out any testing, allow breaks of time (a day or so, for example, if the total project duration allows this) between developing a page and then testing it (or arrange for prototyped items to be tested/evaluated by someone other than the developer) so that you can experience them from a fresh point of view. Full testing is completed as a separate subsequent step (Step 11) later, but initial testing is needed here as part of the prototyping process.

The series of prototyping cycles for a webpage is judged to be complete when the page is tested and evaluated as being acceptable and complete. Throughout this process, be sure to make regular backups of your work and keep archived versions as planned (i.e., as planned in Step 7 of the overall process).

A few new items of documentation have been briefly mentioned in the paragraphs above – let's look at them in a little more detail.

Summaries of the changes made during the prototyping iterations are documented as 'prototyping innovations' (see Table 8.3). This list makes it easier to keep track of design changes made due to the prototyping cycle and how the main design documentation might be affected. In the first column, the name of the original design documentation (that relates to the design item changed) and any reference numbers applicable (including the version number of the documentation item) are stated.

Table 8.3: Prototyping innovations

Original Documentation Name/ID	Summary of Changes or Additions Made (include diagrams if needed)
Screen layout and webpage dialogue for main page (index.htm)	Each icon (one for each religion) made into mouse rollovers – image changing to a picture relevant to the religion in question
Web dialogue (Judaism page)	Now the audio file is downloaded on mouse click (not streamed)
Screen layouts (all pages)	Background colours – changed to a consistent pastel purple

Prototyping Innovations	
Website ID:	World Religions
Date:	Weeks 8/9
Initials:	FK

Brief details explaining what changes or additions were made to the substance of the original documentation are given in Column 2 (including visualisation of the changes if this helps – possibly extended on a separate sheet). The website ID is stated at the foot of the table. Table 8.3 (Prototyping innovations) serves as an easy reference for checking any wider impacts and in case we need to trace back the way a design has evolved (e.g., if the new idea doesn't work very well and changes need to be 'unpicked').

Table 8.4: Initial feedback comments

Webpage Item	Comments	Action
1.Prayer link on Judaism page	Doesn't connect to audio	Check if link correct, streaming operational
2.Text links on each detailed page	Not easy to see, and don't look that impressive	To be considered
3.Page background colours	Page colours look a bit 'loud'	Try different colours and vary for each page

Initial Feedback Comments	
Website /page name:	World Religions/index.htm
Prototype version no.:	1
Feedback participants:	FK/target user
Date:	Weeks 8/9

The 'initial feedback comments' form (Table 8.4) is where we document comments by the developers/users maki ng the tests on the latest prototype version of the webpage. If there are any positive or negative comments/observations made, then make a note of the relevant webpage item and a summary of the comment or observation. If any action is perceived to be needed and can be suggested, then make notes on that in the third column. The webpage name and the prototype version number (each new prototype should be given a version number), the date, and participant details (for the purposes of any necessary followup discussions) should be included. Examples of feedback are included in Table 8.4. They are items that might have been recorded during the iteration immediately preceding the one addressed by Table 8.3. Hence the feedback items contribute to the innovations explored in the next iteration.

As with all other elements of the documentation described in these chapters, the use of electronic copies of the tables make it easier to expand them for whatever detail is needed (i.e., expand the depth of each row and/or increase the number of rows).

Table 8.5: Testing during build results

	Purpose	**Usability**	**Aesthetics**
Problem	1. Audio streaming not working on Judaism page	1. Text links on each detailed page are not easy to see/use	1. The background colour on pages is too bright – need something to help calmness and thoughtfulness 'atmomosphere'
Resolution	1. Try correcting link and streaming setup, or could use download technique	1. Possibly larger font, could use graphic buttons or imagery for links	1. Try a pastel colour, perhaps a shade of purple/ blue
Problem			
Resolution			
Problem			
Resolution			
Testing During Build Results **Webpage project ID:** World Religions **Date:** Week 8/9			

Any problems uncovered from the initial feedback, and resolutions to those problems, should be recorded in Table 8.5 (Testing during build results), identifying if the problem is purpose, usability, or aesthetics related. Summary details of each problem found (and the associated action that resolves the problem) are placed in the table. Table 8.5 illustrates a few example problems (as discovered in the testing during the same iteration covered by Table 8.4) and resolutions that are envisaged based on our case study. The date and the relevant website project ID should be stated at the foot of the form.

Exercises

Seminar Topics

1. "I know this project so well now, I don't need to do any more documenting". Discuss the extent to which you empathise with this sentiment.
2. Discuss the 'webpage build cycle' (Fig. 8.1.). For example, do you think it would be equally effective whatever order the pages are developed and/or if pages are developed in parallel? Identify any problems/issues.
3. If copyright clearance is not given for an item (e.g., an image), what might one do to resolve the situation?

Tutorial Exercises

1. List the documentation you would use as input to tasks in this step and the items of documentation you should work with (i.e., to add/edit information) in this step.
2. What are the distinct purposes of the following two pieces of documentation – the 'initial feedback comments' and the 'prototyping innovations' tables?
3. Give five examples you would include as components of a webpage (in the 'aspect/items build list').

Case Study

1. Write a few short paragraphs to list which software you are going to use, any plans to gain skills, and about the sequence for carrying out the various project tasks.
2. Prioritise and place your webpages into the order in which they need to be created. Synchronise this with content/ capture planning.
3. Complete an 'aspect/items build list' for each webpage. Work through the documentation, the building, and the testing needed for this step, completing the various design documentation items as you progress with the prototyping.

8.2 Step 11: Website Testing and Evaluation

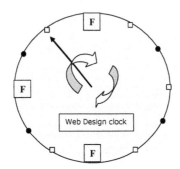

The eleventh hour has arrived. The time has come for full testing. This step has the main purpose of confirming the extent to which the designed and implemented website matches the design requirements. Ideally, all the desired usability, aesthetics, and purpose characteristics should be satisfied by the design features. The testing is not likely to reveal very many nasty surprises, as the whole project process followed so far has been based on maintaining the close connection between design decisions and requirements. To have reached this stage means that several steps have already been completed where website needs and related design ideas have iteratively and painstakingly been identified, specified, and implemented.

In this step, the task is to formally and thoroughly double-check the appropriateness and effectiveness of the implemented website design. In effect, it is a 'rubber stamping' of the previous careful work on the project. The thoroughness of this final project activity may uncover some weaknesses, and this will only serve to further strengthen the overall project outcome.

It is essential that the developer, or the main developer if there is a development team, prepare the test plan and the test results documentation ready for completion, as they will have the most comprehensive perspective and awareness of the details of the implementation. The testing itself (and the reporting of the test results) is ideally carried out by someone else – someone in a better position to give an independent and 'fresh' view who is not directly involved in the frontline of the development work and/or possibly from a different project team. In this way, there is less risk of familiarity overshadowing sensitivity and more chance that the fresh view will uncover anything that remains to be uncovered. The chosen person has to be able to analyse design documentation and assess the mapping of the design ambitions and needs to the implemented website. If the website is very large, it may in fact need several people to share the testing and evaluation task.

Some of the checking relies on objective opinions being concluded, even though many aspects involve subjective judgment. This is inescapable, as website requirements and designs can have elements that are difficult to specify in an absolute finite way, and human perception is not an exact science. Also, as implementations can vary considerably and yet satisfy needs equally well, there has to be flexibility in recognising and assessing the appropriateness of designs.

This testing step can be considered as having two main facets. First is the testing and verification of the features and processes implemented in the website design. We check that all the documentation design features exist in the implementation, and then they are all checked to see if everything 'works' (in a practical, pragmatic sense). We need to test whether link buttons or text links, for example, successfully take us to the intended display, page, or item when clicked. We need to test every intended interaction, process, and autoload action in our website carefully and thoroughly.

Next is the testing and verification of the extent to which the desired purpose, usability, and aesthetic characteristics are achieved by the designed and implemented website. This second strand of testing requires us to make an assessment of the extent to which the implemented processes, and designs around these processes, collectively support the achievement of the site's aspirations in terms of purpose, usability, and aesthetics. So this strand involves *perception* – in this case, making a judgment whether the targeted design aspirations seem to have been effectively satisfied by the implemented design ideas (i.e., are the actual deliverables and impact on the user consistent with the balance of purpose, aesthetics, and usability envisaged?). For some aspects of the website, this may be quite difficult (e.g., in terms of involving high levels of subjective judgment), and for others it will be more straightforward.

The evaluator or evaluators need to have access to all of the existing design documentation, with particular attention given to the website scenario statement, navigation designs, screen layouts, purpose maps, and webpage dialogue sheets, together with the three tables specifying the purpose, usability, and aesthetic targets with the associated specific design ideas.

To document the plan and the results of the testing, Table 8.6 (Existence/action/interaction testing) and the purpose, usability and aesthetic design tables (initiated in Steps 4 and 5) are utilized.

The 'existence/action/interaction testing' form (Table 8.6) is used to represent what is being tested (and expected outcomes) and record the results of the testing. There should be a separate sheet or set of sheets for each webpage. Each sheet has space for up to nine separate items to be tested (one column for each test), but as webpages will often have a greater number of items, actions, and interactions, more than one sheet may be needed for particular webpages.

There should be a column completed for each item that is expected on the webpage – i.e., that is subject to a user action, or simply 'exists' on the page, and any aspect event that occurs 'automatically' (e.g., on 'page load'). It will often be the case that an item is subject to two or more possible user actions, and each has to be represented and tested (two columns are best used, but the test recording could be merged into one column to save some space and time). If the same action has two expected outcomes, the two tests can be represented in two columns if this helps clarity. Some of the boxes will be left blank, with only the appropriate one being ticked or completed for the relevant case in question.

Notice that there are some blank action type boxes on the form. These are for any additional user actions that are not preprinted in the table (you need to state the action type in that empty box). Please also note the action termed 'none'. This action type allows us to include items in the test plan that are being tested purely for presence on the page, or background processing perhaps – i.e., not involving any specific user action. The details of the 'happening', and how and when it occurs, are given in the 'auto (info)' box on the form. Some aspects (e.g., the extraction of a system date for later display) to be tested are not visible but are coded processes that need to be checked for functionality. Other aspects that would be represented by 'none'/'auto info' include checks for the simple presence of webpage content items. Discretion is needed for these in terms of whether to use separate columns for content items or group items into the same column.

Table 8.6: Existence/action/interaction testing

Existence/Action/Interaction Testing Form									
Item / Action	1	2	3	4	5	6	7	8	9
Item name	Icon menu								
Actions Click	X								
Double click									
Mouse-over									
Mouse-out									
Mouse other									
Selection									
View									
None									
Auto (info)									
Expected outcome	Each new page opens in main page								
Tested ok?	Y								
Comments/ planned solutions									
Webpage name/ID: Main page/World Religions **Evaluator's name:** FK **Date:** Weeks 10/11									

The webpage dialogue documentation is the main source for details of the interaction aspects that have to be included in this testing. Navigation designs, purpose maps, the content index, and screen layouts are the other main documentation items acting as inputs to complete Table 8.6.

The test designer should present the test plan documentation to the evaluator with every column completed except for the 'tested ok?' and 'comments/planned solutions' sections. The latter box would typically be used if the test was unsuccessful and/or something was noticed by the evaluator that needs to be drawn to the attention of the development team. This means that, during the actual testing, documentation completion is quite swift, but time is needed by the development team to prepare the test documentation, which in effect represents a test plan. This testing ascertains whether all operational/interface design elements as specified in the website design are present and work as expected. Table 8.6 shows one example test item and result (mouse-click selection of icons in a menu). Outcomes of the testing are examined in the subsequent step (Step 12).

A second mode of testing is needed in addition to those above. It is necessary to consider the extent to which the consequences of the collective design items satisfy the targeted purpose, usability, and aesthetic characteristics.

To do this, we go back to the purpose aspirations, usability planning, and aesthetics planning tables (initially completed in Steps 4 and 5). It is necessary to initially test if each design idea stated in Column 6 of these tables has been implemented. This is done for each of the purpose, usability, and aesthetic tables. Put a 'Y' in the appropriate column (Column 7) to show that the idea has now been implemented. If not, then brief comments are needed at the foot of the table to identify if the particular design idea is in fact needed or is now to be excluded from the design, and any special action needed. Secondly, the evaluator has to decide if the purpose, usability, and aesthetic design targets are all sufficiently addressed by the implemented design ideas. Awareness of target audience needs, characteristics, and expectations, as well as the desirable purpose, usability, and aesthetic attributes, is very important in this difficult but crucial task. Column 4 is used to indicate this judgment (Y/N). Again, if the answer is 'no', then comments are needed at the foot of the table to expand on any action to be taken. If there are any items that are high priority and have not been sufficiently satisfied, then ideas for improving the design are very much needed and should be flagged for attention in the next Review and Reflect step (Step 12).

In Chapter 3 (p. 50 onwards), there is a discussion of heuristics that can be utilised in the evaluation of website usability. These heuristics can play a part at this point in the project in assessing the effectiveness of the usability design.

Exercises

Seminar Topics

1. Discuss any differences between 'testing' and 'evaluation'.
2. Discuss the possibility of making *one* of the two modes of testing (i.e., 'existence/action/interaction' using Table 8.6 and 'purpose/usability/aesthetics') a clear priority. Analyse the potential problems and impacts.
3. Consider any differences there might be between test results where the tester/evaluator is a) a developer of the item(s) tested and b) a nondeveloper of the items.

Tutorial Exercises

1. What are the two main types of testing that need to be done when evaluating an implemented website?
2. Give five examples of items/objects that might appear in Table 8.6 ('Existence/action/interaction testing'), plus any more action categories that you can think of that do not appear on the form already.
3. What design documentation is used as input to this step? Name two items that are particularly important.

Case Study

1. Consider and list which aspects of your website you feel might be unsuccessful when you go through the testing of the website in this step.
2. Make a list of what you regard as being the 'minimum' outcome of the testing for you to feel that the website is in a satisfactory condition for going 'live'?
3. Fully test your website and record the results using the documentation as described in this step.

8.3 Step 12: User Evaluation/Review and Reflect (3)

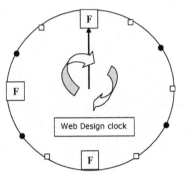

This is the 'final hour' of the design and development process, the final stage of the project, where time is taken for user evaluation of the site and to review and reflect on its effectiveness and appropriateness.

As in previous Review and Reflect steps, there is the option for flashbacks to earlier steps, and this is where any necessary finishing touches would be identified and applied to the website design. Finally, a decision has to be made to declare whether the website is satisfactory in terms of completeness and effectiveness – i.e., ready to go 'live'.

Crucially, user representatives are fully involved in this evaluation, contributing to a fully participative final review and reflection on the condition of the website. As with the previous Review and Reflect (R&R) steps, this step has the purpose of studying and evaluating requirements, decisions, designs, design ideas, and test results, plus any related issues that urgently need to be resolved. This final R&R step carries with it extra responsibilities, as the aim is to establish if everything possible has now been done to arrive at a complete, balanced website with an optimum mix of purpose, aesthetics, and usability characteristics.

In this final Review and Reflect step, it is necessary for key user representatives to combine with the website developer, or the development team, to focus on the following:

- appraising design needs and ideas for satisfying those needs;
- how well the implemented design is succeeding in matching target purpose, usability, and aesthetic desires;
- project plan – deadlines, costs, and unresolved problems;
- study of the website, testing documentation, and, where needed, associated design documentation to identify and address unresolved gaps, anomalies, and conflicts;
- user evaluation of the implemented website.

A thorough and skilful application of the previous steps in the website design process will make it very likely that the website now is in a very strong and very satisfactory condition. Hence, although a crucial step, it should be the case that little new work is needed at this point – reaping the benefits of all of the previous comprehensive work in the specification, design, building, and testing/evaluating phases of the project. However, it is possible that errors and omissions could be identified and that they may need to be addressed and rectified before final implementation. The test documentation from the previous step is one major input, together with new evaluations of the site carried out by user/client representatives. The users/clients will have their own 'natural' perspectives on expectations and perceptions of how well the website matches those expectations. The test results documentation (as shown in Table 8.6) illustrates the development team's view on any issues that need addressing. The key elements of the rest of the BWD design documentation are available with clarifying any issues and with resolving any problems.

The procedure for this current step is similar to Review and Reflect (1 and 2) and comprises a mixture of individual analysis and group discussion/analysis of the implemented website and the associated designs. The R&R report (Table 8.7) is used to list any items that are identified as needing new or additional work. Progress on the items is also recorded. The report format is as used in previous R&R steps, and an example completed R&R report can be seen in Chapter 6 (Step 6).

The table helps to organise the outcome of evaluations so that the 'problems' are clearly identified and that the required action is detailed and its completion monitored. The report operates like a 'sign-off' checklist sheet, whereby a list of items is built up that need attention, what we feel needs to be done is noted, and progress on resolution plans can be recorded.

The 'Item' column should state simply the specific aspect that has been identified as not yet being completed or unsatisfactorily completed. The 'Source' column is used to indicate which part of the website is involved (and details of directly associated pieces of design documentation that particularly define the item in question).

The 'Comments/Action' column needs to clearly define the problem and suggest a remedy if possible, and make it clear who is to take the necessary action to resolve the issue. The final column is used to record any successful resolution of the issue and/or if it is deemed acceptable or necessary to accept the problem without delaying the website's 'going live'.

Table 8.7: R&R report

Item	Source	Comments/ Action	Successfully Resolved Date and Solution
R&R Report **Website ID:** **Direct input to this report** **(documentation items):** **Date:** **BWD Step (6, 9, or 12):**			(template)

Individuals or small groups who have the responsibility to address a problem item need to use whatever information and resources are available. Information could be from existing documentation and/or from further analysis of the situation, and resolution of problems might need the benefit of revisiting a previous step (i.e., a flashback).

It is within this final stage of the process that a point has to be reached where a decision is made whether to fully implement the website onto the Internet for it to go 'live'. The point will possibly be governed by a commercially or market-led deadline, and the project planning would have been working towards this date. Ideally, this deadline will coincide with the point at which the developer/client team is completely satisfied with the quality and appropriateness of the website – with no more need for flashbacks to correct or resolve any problems or deficiencies. The allocation of this decision-making responsibility would have been decided early in the project (in Step 1, Chapter 5).

In Chapters 9 and 10 (Section 3: Implementation Issues), we discuss the topics of 'software tools', in relation to website design and development, and website hosting and management. An important aspect of the latter chapter, and at the heart of the whole book, is that website design is 'alive'. It has a lifetime, a lifetime of needs, and needs that require close and careful attention and nurturing.

Exercises

Seminar Topics

1. Discuss whether some types of websites are likely to be more difficult to design and implement in such a way that all requirements are completely satisfied.
2. Analyse the extent to which *user* evaluation is likely to produce findings that differ from evaluation by developers.
3. What would be your criteria for deciding whether a website is 'finished' and can go 'live'?

Tutorial Exercises

1. Name at least two aspects that are particularly important to address in this R&R step.
2. On what basis should the users/clients judge if website items are satisfactory and acceptable?
3. How do we 'track' progress on problematic aspects revealed in this step?

Case Study

1. Gather all the documentation, including the test results, that you have produced so far in your project to be ready as reference material during the evaluation of the website.
2. Arrange for user/client representatives for your project to help evaluate your website.
3. Decide whether the website implementation is now complete and at an acceptable level of quality, and, if necessary, work on resolving issues (e.g., utilising flashbacks) until a decision can be made to 'go live'.

Section 3: Implementation Issues

CHAPTER NINE

Software Tools

Overview

This chapter takes a look at currently available software typically used in website implementation projects. The design and development process described in this book is formulated so that it can be followed and utilised with whatever software and hardware environment is being used for the website development. However, this chapter is included here to give general guidance regarding software typically in use and indicates any issues that might need to be faced when choosing and using the software technology in the context of the website design process. It includes consideration of software suitable for accommodating database and mobile technology requirements in the website design.

The quoted examples of packages should not be construed as being specific recommendations, as equivalent packages offered by other vendors would also be applicable. There are also numerous alternatives available via the Web as freeware or shareware downloads via the many download portal websites.

Give and Gain

This chapter needs you to give about 35 minutes to read it, plus time for the exercises at the end, and it will help you gain the following important aspects:

- an awareness of the range of software available and required to help with the process of designing and implementing websites;
- guidance in selecting software for your project;
- an introduction to the special requirements relating to database and mobile technology website projects.

You need to read this chapter if you are new to the task of designing and implementing websites or you need to refresh your knowledge of current and emerging website technology available for use in your project.

Introduction

The details of the software that you will use in your website project will depend on many factors and often will not necessarily be decided on grounds that achieve maximum operational effectiveness. For example, software can be costly and can be time consuming to learn, so this has to be considered when looking around at the various possibilities and evaluating the bigger picture'. Commencement on a project may need to be speedy, so there might not be time for detailed evaluation of software choices. For expediency, a project might need to adopt the most convenient and speedy option, regardless of any possible disadvantages.

The following sections indicate the range of activities and tasks that are needed in typical website projects and describe examples of appropriate software available in the marketplace. Guidance is given with regard to how you might select from the available software.

Selection Criteria

For website development projects, software would tend to be needed for the following activities:

- Project management
- Requirements analysis
- Detailing design/prototyping
- Content creation/acquisition
- Code building/prototyping
- Media streaming/presentation
- Special features (e.g., databases and mobile technology)
- Testing

As in any computer-based application development project, there are factors that need to be identified and compared in order to ascertain the best choices in project software.

In all cases there is a common set of criteria that can be used in selecting software to support these activities. The following list of components collectively forms the basis for making decisions. Each situation of course will present its own unique set of circumstances, and decisions will need to be made in that given context.

- Costs
    - o Learning time/skills acquisition
    - o Task completion time
    - o Cost of software license(s) and installation
    - o Any necessary hardware updates
    - o Integration (other software/hardware)
    - o 'Version updating'

- Benefits
    - o Creative/technical possibilities
    - o Efficiency/performance
    - o Marketable profile
    - o Fit with existing skills/systems

- Miscellaneous
    - o Technical support
    - o Standability

In effect, what any project leader and website developer is looking for is the optimum situation whereby the software

- is easy and swift to learn and use,
- suits the required functionality/scope,
- matches the available budget,
- is very compatible with other software chosen for the project,
- has no difficulties with respect to installation, integration, and technical operation, and
- opens up interesting possibilities (software characteristics can inspire new project ideas).

It will often be the case that there is neither the time nor the inclination to analyse all of these components very deeply and form a total picture of the pros and cons of the various types of software. Often the decisions have to be very swift (due to the immediacy of beginning a project, for example) and can be driven by immediate needs, marketing hype/each, personal preferences, budgets, and/or convenience. It is still a very fast-growing and progressing sector of IT activity, and decisions have to keep pace with associated demands of developers, clients, and the marketplace.

However, speedy decisions and appropriations can be very regrettable, causing long-lasting problems. It is preferable that the management of a project include the monitoring of the effectiveness of software and processes being utilised. It is still the case – and in fact as hardware and software costs tend to fall relatively, it is increasingly the case – that the cost of personnel time (salaries and employment costs) is the highest element of a project's total cost. The ability to quickly and effectively implement websites if and when the need arises is very valuable. Therefore a change of software can make a big difference to a project team if it means that subsequent progress is more effective and efficient.

Project Management

Step 2 of the process described in this book addresses the aspect of implementing procedures to manage the development of the project. Every website design project should adopt at least a basic level of project management:

- breaking down the whole project into a list of specific tasks;

- scheduling a sequence for the completion of the tasks, including any tasks that could be completed simultaneously and tasks that need other tasks to be completed in advance;
- allocating people to complete each task;
- having a system for monitoring progress and making decisions about amending original resourcing and scheduling where necessary.

To an extent, the 'inhouse' procedures at the organisation will determine the details and depth of the project management approach. For medium to large projects, it is beneficial to have a dedicated project manager to take the responsibility for what is an important aspect of the whole project. Meeting deadlines is often crucial to the success of a project, as is the delivery of a satisfactorily completed project on budget. Having a person whose sole responsibility is to ensure that a project follows a development plan and controls the difficult task of monitoring progress and applying contingencies significantly reduces the risk of shortfalls in the outcomes.

It is quite possible to conduct project management without the aid of specialist software (e.g., MS Project), although electronic means of some kind (e.g., a wordprocessing package) are almost mandatory to ease updates and access to the design information. Typical graphical techniques in project management are drawing Gantt charts (to show the sequence of all project tasks) and carrying out network analysis (to enable a critical path of tasks to be identified). Both of these techniques help in guiding decision making as well as providing a visual plan for project tasks. Word-processing or visual presentation packages (e.g., MS PowerPoint, Adobe Photoshop) or specialised project management software can be used. Project management software can also provide quite sophisticated help with 'what if' analysis and in managing both the financial and practical dimensions of a project.

It is of the utmost importance that the project management be carried out not as an administrative exercise but as a fundamental part of the project process. An attractive set of charts and lists will not necessarily make for a successful implementation, but the thorough use of project management to ensure that the tasks needed to effectively complete all the design and implementation will go a long way towards achieving project success.

It follows then that project management skills are required, with software (and software skills) a secondary step to implementing those skills. Decisions on the extent of project management procedures to adopt and if and what software to utilise need to be made in advance of commencing any actual project tasks, so that software can be put in place. Software skills may also need to be acquired.

In the website design process described in this book, it is at each Review and Reflect step that the project management position is formally examined, but project management is in effect an ongoing activity within and throughout the whole development process.

Requirements Analysis

The methodology for website design and implementation described in Section 2 guides the ascertaining of the requirements and checking and monitoring their achievement. We now deal with the options available regarding software suitable for these tasks.

The process described in Section 2 includes the following in documenting the requirements analysis (please refer to Chapter 5, Steps 1 and 3, and also back to charts introduced in Chapter 2):

- Website design context framework
- Website genre subtypes
- Website user characteristics
- Website scenario statement
- Project attributes
- Questionnaire/interview sheets
- Analysis meetings forms
- Website design requirements list
- Purpose/aesthetics/usability tables

All of the sheets/forms can be printed out from the book's website, ready for completion in your project, and/or downloaded as templates for you to use electronically.

Typical packages to utilise for working with the forms are Microsoft Word or Adobe Acrobat writer. It would also be possible to use packages such as Adobe Photoshop or Microsoft PowerPoint, but simple word processing is quite adequate. All of the forms in the documentation used in this book are designed so that where a project needs more space in a particular part of the documentation (to describe or define something) the tables can be expanded to accommodate the necessary information. For this reason, it is much more flexible and effective to work with the documentation in electronic form (rather than handwrite it onto printed templates). This approach also makes it much easier to make updates and distribute the documentation via the Web or an intranet). Version control is important and is made more manageable by careful naming of all files (including using version numbers in the filenames).

Meetings with clients and potential users (to help ascertain the requirements for the website) will inevitably vary in nature, ranging from formal committee or board meetings to informal onetoone discussions in offices and/or at the computer. This will mean that a variety of techniques and technology will be needed to gather and record the primary data, with later reformatting and transfer to the web design documentation forms. Simple handwritten notes are often used and sometimes accompanied by audio and/or video recording of the sessions. Naturally, all permissions for making the recordings are needed, as there may be sensitivity to this aspect and there could be requests for notes to be taken rather than making electronic recordings.

Detailed Design/Prototyping

The creation of the layout and structural design of the webpages, and of the website overall, is usually carried out in three stages: sketching out ideas, prototyping design ideas, and progressively building up the details of the website content around that design.

This section deals with the design ph ase of the project and the software that is typically useful in the design tasks, including any design prototyping. As with all of the other projec t phases, wordprocessing software is useful here, essentially for completing the text (and simple diagrammatic) project documentation.

For screen layout design, some pe ople like to begin prototyping the screen layouts electronically alongside paperbased drawings, with the view that it helps the users/clients recognise and associate with the designs more easily. It also provides a useful basis for the subsequent coding stage. The immediate choice of software for screen layout prototyping is likely to be the software planned to be used in the later codingbuilding phase of the project. However, it could be the case that the people with those software skills are not available at this earlier stage. There is also the argument for keeping design prototyping deliberately separate from the programming in the implementation environment. In these cases, it would be typical to use applications such as image software (e.g., Adobe Photoshop, Fireworks), scene-based software (such as Macromedia Director or Flash), or desktop publishing software such as Adobe InDesign. In this way, visual/layout designers can get to work in 'graphic design' environments without the possible complexities and unfamiliarity of working with HTML coding/building packages. Often, these packages make for easier demonstration to users and easier prototyping.

For situations where design prototyping in the 'development' environment is preferred, there are several options available. Most popular software operates on Mac and PC platforms (although there are some interface design and detailed functionality differences). Software that can enable designs to be prototyped, with the designs directly forming the base code for full implementation later, includes Macromedia Dreamweaver and Microsoft FrontPage. These packages are very powerful in that a visual interface is used (together with a large range of selectable options via menus and lists) to form the required design, with the associated HTML code being automatically generated. HTML is the code that is used by the Internet browsers to control presentation and handling of the website (the exceptions being situations where new media software such as Flash is being used to form a complete website). The code generated tends to be rather voluminous, but this usually does not significantly impact efficiency of operation, and any small loss here is massively offset by the power and flexibility offered by the packages. A 'learning curve', however, which can be quite substantial depending on the complexity of design demanded by the design ideas and on the existing skills and experience of the developers.

An alternative approach is to use a simple text editor (such as Notepad, TextPad, or SimpleText) to prototype the design. In this case, all of the HTML code (or HTML code, if JavaScript/Cascading Style Sheets are not present) is formed manually. The task is eased by developing blocks of code that can be reused (using 'copy and paste' from an existing file to a new website project). Manually building the code can be a very effective method, giving maximum flexibility and control over the details of the implementation, speedy editing, and easy reuse of the code. It does, however, require specialist skills, and possibly it is not quite so easy to ensure consistency of styling between parts of the system (compared with using HTML-generating software) and often not so easy for new/replacement developers to maintain previously completed code.

A further alternative is to utilise GUI 'webpage creating' software that is associated with popular browsers and/or wordprocessing packages. This approach is mostly only effective and satisfactory for small and simple websites, as the range of stylistic control over the details of the design is not usually as powerful as when using specialist code-generating software or manually created code using a text editor. However, using such packages as Word and Netscape Navigator to create webpages does have the advantage that there is wide familiarity with the software interface and how it operates.

If (D)HTML coding is used in design   prototyping, then browsers will be needed to view the prototyped designs (e.g., Internet Explorer, Netscape, Firefox).

Ahead of creating prototype webpages and/or webpage layouts, it is necessary to build up a reasonably comprehensive set of design information. This book describes documentation ranging from simple lists of requirements through purpose/usability/aesthetics needs and design definitions, screen layout designs, navigation maps, and webpage dialogue designs. All of this design documentation work can be done using standard wordprocessing packages such as Microsoft Word. Templates are available (from the book's website) that can be used as a basis for the documentation. It is recommended that the designers themselves complete this documentation and work on it as the website design process unfolds, as the act of specifying the design in the documentation becomes part of the design process itself (and often helps to improve the design due to further considerations being made whilst crystallising and detailing the information).

Content Creation/Acquisition

The content of a website – i.e., all the text, images, graphics, and multimedia – have to be acquired, prepared from existing material, and/or created.

In parallel with the design task, it is usually very worthwhile to be gathering and developing the content information – text, pictures, graphics, video, audio, etc. Clearly, these stages are likely to involve several people and several sources of information, material, and agreement. As with all other aspects of a website project, the management of the process is important to make sure that content procured is appropriate, accurate, complete, 'of the right style', and timely, and to make sure that the design of how that information is presented and navigated is effective and as desired. Copyright freedom or approval for all items needs to be in place.

The acquisition of new material to be used as, or in the creation of, media content will require appropriate hardware and devices (as well as media software that has 'capture' facilities). This could typically include DV cameras, digital still cameras, microphones, and portable recorders. Analog equipment would also need appropriate 'capture card' boards to be present (or their equivalent) as an interface to the computer. Most computers have firewire or USB interfaces that enable easy transfer of digital media material to the computer. Conversion hardware is needed for analog input.

The required 'creative' time and skills (e.g., for new writing and/or audio/video) need to be identified and scheduled so that the items created are ready for use when needed. These tasks could be subcontracted to specialists outside of the immediate development team.

The content of a website is an absolutely key aspect of a successful website – quality, relevant, and interesting material is crucial. The content needs to be continually assessed for updating and refreshing opportunities so that the website remains of interest, of value, and actively used.

In all cases, some use of multimedia creation/editing software is likely to be needed, although some websites will not have the need for some multimedia components (e.g., audio, video, pictures, and graphics). Training in how to use the software to take full advantage of multimedia content and yet keep file sizes (and hence download times) to a minimum is important. One feature is to consider splitting still images into components (according to whether parts of the images are more suited to certain image/compression types) and saving them in the most appropriate formats (e.g., GIF, JPG, etc.). This can reduce total page file size considerably. Audio and video files must be compressed and have short clip lengths (to keep download times low). 'Midi' can be used for some sounds/music. This format (simple data *describing* sounds) uses very small files, but sound quality can be limited, and it relies on hardware and software recreating sounds based on the data transmitted. Another key feature is to incorporate 'streaming' of sound and video where possible (material viewed/heard at the same time as a file is being downloaded by means of just enough data being placed in a buffer before commencing presentation of the material).

Some popular examples of media software are given below, but please note that this list is not exhaustive and is illustrative rather than being any form of recommendation for use.

Image/graphics:
- Macromedia Flash
- Adobe Photoshop
- Macromedia Freeworks

Sound:
- Cubase (audio and midi)
- Soundforge
- CoolEdit (PC)
- Peak (Mac)
- Goldwave (PC)
- MakingWaves (PC) – audio and midi
- Sound Studio (Mac)

Video:
- Final Cut Pro (Mac)
- Adobe Premiere
- VideoWave (PC)
- Imovie (Mac)

Animation:
- Flash
- Director
- Gif animators

Each multimedia software package has its own set of learning curve difficulties, but some of the packages in the list above need much more familiarisation and training time than others (e.g., Final Cut Pro, Adobe Premiere, Cubase, Flash, Freeworks). This is partly due to their comparatively greater richness in capabilities and complexities available to the designer. It becomes very important in the software selection phase to very clearly recognise the level of needs that is required in the project (as opposed to grossly underusing very powerful, expensive, and time-consuming software). The lists above are placed   roughly in order of complexity and difficulty in quickly learning them. The items nearer the top of the lists in most cases offer more complexity, choices, and control of the editing and creation of the multimedia product. Some design situations only require the simple work that can be carried out using the simpler software and would benefit from adoption of that software. If the packages stated are only found on one platform, this is indicated in parentheses. It is good practice to have several options available to the team and for designers to be sufficiently skilled in a range of multimedia software, which then makes it much more possible to pick and choose environments according to the details of each project. Content management software (e.g., CMS) can be used to help manage and control what could be a rapidly and comprehensively changing process of updating content for a website.

Code Building/Prototyping

The building of the final implemented website involves integrating the prepared content (text, imagery, sound, etc.) into webpages and linking the pages together to form a site.

Websites are usually built in two main ways – using a 'scene based' package (e.g., Macromedia Flash) or using a HTML based approach. HTML pages can be coded directly using a text editor (e.g., Notepad) or utilising code generating packages such as Dreamweaver.

Each environment ostensibly can result in the same level of professional finish' and range of content, and the outcomes mainly depend on the skills of the practitioner, experience using that software environment, and the efforts made to design interesting styles, interfaces, and content material into the website. A key factor is previous experience with each of the software environments – either specifically in the target packages or if there are skills in similar packages. One issue is confidentiality of the coding and materials used in the pages. Using packages such as Flash makes it easier to protect against copying of individual items used in a website. This type of website, however, relies on target users of the website having browsers that include the appropriate player plugins. HTML websites have their own 'compatibility' problems, though, as different browsers (and versions of browsers) process aspects such as JavaScript and Cascading Style Sheets (CSS) in different ways. HTML websites often include the use of Flash or similar multimedia presentations, and so the issue of player plugin compatibility arises again.

There are some situation factors that, especially if time and budgets are short, will influence the choice of software type and specific package:

- experience/skills of the developers;
- client preferences;

- presence of existing software licenses;
- environments used for clients' associated websites;
- presence of content material and interface objects in formats that suit a particular environment;
- good/bad experiences of software in the prototyping phase of the project.

If time and budget allow, and if none of the factors above are very clear, then a broader and open evaluation can take place. If there is little time for evaluation and no substantial existing software skills/experience, it is likely that a project would benefit from using a HTML-generating software package, so this definitely should be included in the evaluation. This approach brings the advantages of consistent and effective websites, robustness, good speed of development, and a useful range of design features to utilise, and learning curves tend to be reasonable.

When it is time for webpages and a website to be tested in place on the Internet, then files need to be transferred onto a webserver. This is carried out using file transfer protocol (FTP) software. Some HTML-generating packages have built-in FTP facilities, but in most cases proprietary FTP software is used (e.g., WS-FTP), which could be full-cost software or freeware/shareware versions. Files can be uploaded and/or downloaded to and from a webserver, and this can be done over an intranet or from remote locations over the Internet.

For testing and evaluating the prototypes, a browser is required – with the necessary media player plugins (e.g., Flash player) so that multimedia content can be successfully experienced with the website. Typically, Internet Explorer and Netscape are used for viewing website prototypes, but other browsers are available. Note that it is important to consider browser version(s), as target audiences might be using older versions than those used in prototyping, revealing incompatibility problems.

Media Streaming/Presentation

Most websites have some amount of digital media content presence. Images and graphics content have been important for several years, and increasingly video and (alone or with video) sound are playing a role. Images and graphics tend to simply be placed on a website for viewing in the normal way, often, though, with some kind of interactive element (e.g., images switching to alternative images on moving the mouse cursor over an image).

Mainly because audio and video files (particularly the latter) can be very large their presentation on a website has to be carefully considered. As broadband connections and transfer rates increase, it is becoming easier to achieve good performance levels with multimedia on websites. Audio/video files (compressed) are often for download on websites. However, it is still useful to utilise streaming, as this technique means that audio and video can be experienced quite efficiently even with modem connections.

Streaming' involves transferring compressed audio and/or video at a steady rate, and once a short time has transpired (enough to fill a buffer' in the client computer with the data), the user can view or listen to the material, hence avoiding delays waiting for complete files to download before beginning viewing/listening. The transferred material can be recorded audio/video, or indeed it can be broadcast' live (a webcast).

The minimum software needed is that necessary to compress the audio/video (otherwise the files will be much too large to successfully stream'). For more robust handling of streaming files and for streaming live webcasts, server' software is best utilised. To view and listen, the website users need the relevant player' software (which when installed has plugins that are used by browsers). Examples are RealMedia, Windows Media, and QuickTime. Each has its own set of producer, server, and player software available for purchase or cutdown versions as freeware.

SMIL (a markup language created from XML) is often used to control the presentation of the media material – e.g., controlling the positioning and timing of various media formats on the screen.

Websites can have digital media that play in players that pop up' externally to a webpage or can be embedded into a page layout. The user of the webpage can be provided with varying degrees of control over the playback. Sound can also be played as background to a viewed page (often using midi format) or in short clips associated with mouse actions.

Special Features

Databases. If a database is used as part of a website implementation, it creates a very powerful scenario. It means that information central to the activities and interests of an organisation or enterprise can be accessed and/or updated via use of the website. Typically used are Microsoft

Access and Oracle, and typically there would be information system packages to maintain the databases offline (e.g., from networked PCs or Macs), with the webpages becoming an alternative interface to the database, providing remote and widespread interaction. There are security issues and technical issues in setting up such a system, and hence this type of website system tends to be associated with medium to large organisations.

The software used to build and maintain the database will hence be proprietary database software (e.g., MS Access, Oracle), and the webpages need to be coded using a language such as XML – either using a text editor (such as Notepad) or specialist editor software (e.g., MobileDev, Xyit, Xgen). XML is useful in that it provides an effective way of enabling forms within a webpage into which a user can enter data that are then transmitted to a database stored on the webserver, allowing information from the database to be presented for viewing by the webpage user. XML is often used in conjunction with scripting languages such as ASP to handle the actual extraction and placement of data from and to an external database. An example of an ASP editor software package is Primascript.

XML has an important advantage over data exchange methods commonly used prior to the emergence of XML in that this implementation of a system to exchange and share cor porate data across networks (wide and local) is much cheaper, particularly in terms of hardware and operating software. The low cost is because it is based on a simple markup language and is compatible with most hardware, operation systems, and databases.

As an alternative, very simple information collection and displays can be handled by JavaScript, which is a scripting language also very widely used to create interactivity in webpage designs. JavaScript scripting can be 'server side' or 'client side'. The former opens up more possibilities (e.g., using databases stored on a webserver), and the latter is less powerful but very efficient, as all processing is on the computer running the browser that is viewing the website – the client machine.

Complex and powerful processing of databases with websites can be achieved using scripting languages such as CGI, which has been widely used for several years, and PHP, which has become prominent more recently. These languages can also be used to create 'dynamic' webpage content – i.e., created and formulated 'on the fly'. There are software packages that specialise in working on CGI (e.g., CGI Editor) or PHP (e.g., Editplus), but simple text editors such as Notepad can be used. One issue that needs consideration is that there are different release versions of the scripting, and this can lead to compatibility problems with webservers.

Mobile Technology. Wireless Markup Language (WML) is the language for coding websites to be accessed via mobile phones and was created as one of several markup languages formed using XML (Extensible Markup Language). Mobile phones that are WAP (Wireless Applications Protocol) capable can be used to show content from specially constructed websites. The websites have to be designed so that the content can realistically be uploaded to a mobile phone and be comfortably seen on the small screens available. Typically news, socially centred, and music/entertainment websites are popular types, but the scope is expanding, especially now that multimedia mobile phones are becoming more widespread.

To create the WML website, a simple text editor or specialist WML software can be used. For testing the websites, it can be useful to utilise WAP simulator software on a PC.

Testing

In the full testing phase of a project, there is a need to document the testing and to carry out the testing itself. For documenting, a simple wordprocessing package is adequate. For testing, the essential software is browser software. A variety of browsers should be used and a range of current and older versions included in the testing (to match the likely range of browsers used by the target audience). If the website has design features to cater for users that do not have the correct plugin software, then these situations should be simulated in the testing.

Testing is usually carried out at the various broadband connection levels and also with a modem connection, and hence the relevant hardware and software to run a modem connection are needed together with an account with an ISP (Internet Service Provider). It is useful to try out a range of screen sizes, and also computers having varying levels of technical specification, to reflect the anticipated range of possibilities that might be applicable to target users of the website.

Chapter Exercises

Seminar Topics

1. Discuss the comparative advantages and disadvantages of designing and prototyping in software environments that are different from those planned for the actual development of the website.
2. "I don't like using (DHTML) code-generating software – I like to develop my webpages to be exactly how I want them." Consider this statement and discuss.
3. Conclude what might be the best general approach to *choosing* between possible software for the design/prototype work.

Tutorial Exercises

1. What main options are available regarding software that can help with delivering the code for DHTML pages?
2. List the criteria that can be used to select software for particular tasks.
3. Make a typical list of packages that can effectively help create and edit the following: sound, text, video, images, and graphics (state at least one for each media type).

Case Study

1. Review your case study project – make a comprehensive list of all project tasks that will require software use.
2. Identify exactly which software is to be used to complete each of these activities, including version number details and whether PC, Mac, or other platform.
3. Consider if you feel there are any contentious issues regarding this list – e.g., affecting necessary training, incompatibilities, installation difficulties, etc.

CHAPTER TEN

Website Hosting and Website Management

Overview

In this chapter, an overview is given of the various options available for hosting and promoting websites. The wide array of companies and organisations offering storage and Internet access facilities to websites nowadays is an industry in itself. Within each provider and across the industry, there are numerous combinations of services and options that can be purchased.

The budget allowance for hosting and management of your website will narrow down the choice, but the task of selection is still likely to be time consuming and carry with it some risk. This chapter attempts to help you become aware of the main issues involved in ascertaining what is needed in terms of hosting, understand the range of possibilities open to you, and assist in making the various choices.

Operating a website can be resource intensive and demand a great deal of attention in order to recognise and resolve any technical problems, keep the website up-to-date, develop and enhance the website, and monitor or react to any online communications. This chapter discusses these aspects and highlights important issues.

Give and Gain

This chapter will take about 30 minutes to read, plus time for the exercises at the end, and will help you gain the following:

- an awareness of the wide range of possibilities for hosting websites;
- guidance in selecting hosting characteristics and providers;
- knowledge that contributes to making a plan for effectively dealing with online communications and updating/growing the website.

You need to read this chapter if you are new to the task of implementing websites or your current project is outside the scope of previous websites.

Website Hosting

Introduction

If we want other people to view our website, we must place the website onto a public server. Even if you can use your own PC as a webserver, it is more common to let an Internet Service Provider (ISP) host the site, as this makes it easier, more convenient, and often more cost-effective, and avoids the security issues relating to having a personal computer online and accessible in this way.

A webserver is a computer that is connected to the Internet and that enables access to webpages and their files as stored on that webserver. Most webservers are dedicated to that activity (for security and performance efficiency reasons), but any computer could be set up to act as a webserver. The computer has to be running 24 hours a day, and the operating systems can be any of the main systems in use; for example, Windows, MAC OS) or Unix

Each webserver, as with all computers attached to the Internet, is assigned a unique IP (Internet Prototcol) address. When we connect to the Internet via an ISP, we are given a temporary IP address for that session. A webserver has a permanent IP address, and this (along with an associated unique domain name) is stored on the DNS (Domain Name System Server) database system. When people request to connect to a particular website, a series of DNS servers are interrogated until the physical location of the webserver storing (hosting) the website is found.

There are domain names for websites, too, and these can be purchased (usually for a moderate annual fee) via organisations that organise and manage this aspect. The same companies also often offer hosting and website design services.

Files for a website have to be stored on a webserver in a directory named 'public_html' (or in a subdirectory). The URL (Universal Resource Locator – the address as typed in the location window of a browser) is usually based on the domain name of the webserver hosting the website, but it can be a simpler, more 'marketable' domain name with the technology physically handling connection to the website. The full address used includes as a suffix the access path of the website files but omitting the 'public_html' directory name – e.g., http://www.xyz.com/directory/filename.html.

Files are transferred to a webserver in a variety of ways, but usually it is done remotely over the Internet using FTP (file transfer protocol) software. It can be done using website creation packages such as Dreamweaver and can also be done using standard file management software (and possibly Telnet software if it is a remote connection) if logged on directly to the webserver. The structure of directories and placement of files within those directories have to exactly match the access path structure reflected in the webpage coding and the coded links within those webpages.

Websites that deal with a topic of interest can be found using any one of a number of facilities on the Web known as 'search engines' – e.g., www.yahoo.com or www.google.com. A user types keywords or phrases into a search box and this brings up a list of sites that claim to be related to that key information. This means that a database has to be built up containing lists of keywords/phrases and IP addresses of related websites. Each search engine facility is either supplied with the information (by the website developer/manager) or they often gather this information automatically by using software that accesses websites and extracts salient data for use in the database.

Types of Web Hosting

There are several types of web hosting, and a very large number of organisations regionally and internationally based offering web hosting services. The services often include options such as emailing, the registering of domain names, server side processing (e.g., database processing), and video/audio streaming. In most cases, the services are supplied at commercial rates, but they also can be free' – e.g., the hosted websites might have to carry advertising in the form of pop up' windows in place of a subscription fee.

The types of hosting include the following:

- a personal webserver
- institution based (e.g., university)
- public server
  - free
  - subscription

Personal webservers could be as simple as a hispec PC and give you maximum control and authority over the technology and content/facilities provided, but they have the major disadvantage that you have to take responsibility for implementing the necessary security measures, covering the cost of the Internet connection (which would need to be at broadband level), and setting up the software and hardware for the computer to operate as a server. Licenses for the required software can be quite expensive, partly depending on the number of concurrent users that can be accommodated.

Employees of medium to large organisations often have the opportunity to place webpages on a webserver operated by the organisation. Students at universities and schools also normally have webspace available for their own personal use, usually for websites related to their studies. A further choice is to use public servers. In some situations, they are free' (and often are funded by advertising appearing as pop up' windows on websites carried by the server), advertising, but there is usually a commercial rate charged in the form of a subscription.

Subscription rates are quite competitive, as there are a very wide range of organisations offering the facility. Most of these vendors provide a variety of package solutions – e.g., to include such services as domain name registration, email, database processing, media streaming, online support, website design, etc. The specifications can typically range as follows:

- 50–600 MB storage space
- 1–6 GB data transfer (monthly)
- 20–60 email accounts
- CGI/PHP scripting (yes/no)
- IP support (yes/no)
- Media streaming (yes/no)
- Technical support (high/low)
- 'Online store' facilities (varies in power/extent)

Hosting can be provided on a variety of operating systems (e.g., Windows, Unix/Linux), and the website user will be largely unaware of which operating system is being utilised. There are some technical differences in facilities that can be provided, and some facilities (e.g., specific types of scripting) are not compatible with all platforms, so the selection of hardware/operating system environment can be important.

Guidance on Selection

The choice of hosting type and characteristics of the hosting 'plan' selected has to be driven by the requirements, opportunity, and budget. A personal 'hobby' website clearly has a different set of needs compared with a corporate or other high-profile website, for example. It might be the case that the website owner/client has the opportunity to use institution webspace, and also the available budget will vary. All of these ingredients affect the range of available choices and the details of the selections made.

There are websites that offer advice that can be referenced, and some of these provide statistics and other data (e.g., review ratings of web hosting providers and discussion articles) to help give some objectivity to the selection process (see the book's website for example links).

Apart from the particular technical specifications that you desire (e.g., webspace, monthly bandwidth, etc.), a 'good' website hosting provider should include the following:

- 24 hour support (telephone/online)
- 99% uptime guarantee
- Server backups

- Alternative power supplies
- Highbandwidth Internet connection
- Alternative Internet connection routes

Domain Name Registration

A domain name is a unique name for a website, like www.yahoo.com and www.google.com. A domain name is actually a userfriendly way of humanising' something that is used by the Internet software when handling the accessing of websites and their content – i.e., the domain name acts as an alias to the unique octet IP address of the webpage or webpage component files.

Domain names must be registered and then added to a large domain name register, with information about your site (including your Internet IP address) being stored on a DNS server. A hierarchy of DNS servers is used to enable websites (and files) to be located very effectively and efficiently.

Registration of a domain name is necessary so that we can have useful and uptodate databases listing all existing domain addresses and has to be managed (so that uniqueness and accuracy are controlled). There are numerous companies (mostly operating from websites) that offer domain name registration, and the process is relatively straightforward and speedy. A subscription charge applies for this service, usually annual or biannual.

The first step is to search to see if the desired domain name is available (via online interfaces) either with the preferred domain name extension (e.g., .com, .co.uk, .tv, etc.) or with alternative extensions. The nextstep is to confirm the choice(s) and make the payment. In a short space of time (a few hours in most cases), the domain name is available for use. Often, webspace is also needed and is purchased alongside the domain name, but these can be obtained separately and from different vendors. Traditionally, the extensions of '.com' and a few others have been the most popular and perceived as being the most prestigious, but the newer options (e.g., .tv, .biz, etc.) are becoming more widespread and accepted.

The purpose of a domain name is to attract attention and also to make it easy for potential users to recognise, type in, and remember the domain name. Typically, the best examples of domains have the following characteristics:

- Brief – The shorter your domain, the easier it is to type in (or copypaste), with less chance of typographical errors.

- Meaningful – Choose/create a domain name that relates to your site in a way that people will understand and recognise.
- Clear – Avoid selecting a name that is difficult to spell or pronounce (i.e., make it easy to relay to others by the spoken word).
- Subdomains (e.g., http//store.apple.com) usually do not need registration, as they are set up to be accessible via the registered main domains (e.g., www.apple.com).

Often, free website hosting has the characteristic of there not being a unique domain name used to access the website but a directory within an established domain name. This makes it a cheaper option for the website owner but restrictive in marketing/profile terms.

Site Promotion

A website can only be successful and create the interest, business activity, and/or any other desired reaction if people know it exists and gain access to it. Promotion of the website falls into two main categories – 'real world' and 'Internet/based'. In the real world, we can make use of the following:

- 'Word of mouth' – people being impressed and spreading the news by informal or formal discussions with other people. Nowadays, this would more likely be via email or chatrooms, etc.
- Advertising – press/media articles, advertising space, flyers, posters, mailings.

The Internet offers numerous possibilities, which include:

- links placed on existing websites, including popular 'portals' for links to sites in the genre of your website;
- placing details of the website on email lists and discussion group websites;
- submission of the website URL and keywords to the major search engines used by people on the Web – e.g., yahoo.com, google.com, etc. (n.b. search engines rate websites partly based on the number of links to your website from other sites, so arranging for these links can be very fruitful).

Website Maintenance and Enhancement

Introduction

Websites are living, 'organic' entities and need regular if not constant attention to keep them alive and maintain their relevance and usefulness. The pages might need factual updates (e.g., contact names and addresses, new or changed product specifications, event dates and details, etc.), style 'makeovers', extensions to the scope of content, and general 'news', amongst other possibilities for enhancement. It might be necessary to implement corrections to errors recognised on the site, which could include functionality problems or performance issues.

It also could be the case that the website includes the facility for users of the website to interact by way of communicating to the webmaster (or other contacts) and/or placing material onto the website. All of this will need some level of monitoring and reaction by the website owner or operators.

A key aspect of planning for effective website maintenance and enhancement is to identify who will be responsible for the various actions and overall monitoring and managing of the need for the actions.

Online Communications

It is likely that the website will provide the user with several options for communicating with the organisation running the website and/or specific people associated with the website content. It will have been part of the design process to agree on appropriate modes of communication (e.g., email, phone, snailmail, etc.) and to put in place procedures to make sure that the communications will be processed by the people concerned.

Some of these communications might not prove to be very effective, and so it is useful to have someone appointed to collect emails to general addresses (e.g., for use when direct communications do not work) and also have someone monitoring messages placed on bulletin boards or guestbooks. In some cases, there will be a need to 'mop up' situations where users are in need of more attention and help, and in others the information placed on the website might be 'unsuitable' for publication (e.g., insensitive or illegal) and need to be removed from display.

Effective and timely response to users' communications is a very important component of website planning and can significantly affect the satisfaction and rating of the site.

Take care when providing or encouraging communications and interactions with people and with the site – if it is going to be difficult or impossible to successfully satisfy the demands of such activity, it might be advisable to reduce the scope and hence avoid disappointments and disgruntlement. Good levels of effective communication, however, are a valuable asset to any website.

Website Repair and Growth

In most cases, there will be some instances of errors or omissions being noticed during the early days of a website's use that were not picked up during testing. Those that are identified at this stage could be more a reflection of hindsight or afterthoughts than actual mistakes, but it still means that work is needed to smooth off those rough edges. Prompt attention to these improvements is necessary, so that the overall impact, impression, and effectiveness of the website are not negatively impacted. A good approach is to encourage users to explore and utilise the website extensively in these early days, so that any functionality and/or design problems are revealed as soon as possible.

Websites also need to be kept uptodate in terms of content. Any changes in products, services, or information being presented have to be kept current and accurate. The website might incorporate 'news' items and/or items contributed via user feedback, so this material has to be kept uptodate. Making changes to the website, even if at a 'cosmetic' level, can be a very effective way of keeping a website 'fresh' – maintaining the interest of regular users of the website. Changes might be put in place based on feedback gained from users of the website. Experience and knowledge of the subject matter covered by the website will inevitably progress during the life of the website, and these developments should be reflected in updates.

In addition to these repair and updating activities, as time progresses in the life of a website, the need for enhancement of its scope and depth will probably arise. Most websites need this 'growth' so that they remain 'alive' and relevant as the needs of users and the context of the website evolve. It could be the case that specific elements of the growth were anticipated at the design stage; other aspects will become apparent as time progresses.

A system, then, is needed to enable the needs and possibilities to be reviewed at regular intervals. Unless included in the original project plan, new budgets will need to be established to cover the costs of the work. Agreement on what constitutes maintenance and what constitutes new work can often be a source of conflict between clients and developers, so the boundaries should be made very clear before of the website goes live'.

Documentation

Any changes applied due to website maintenance and enhancement that significantly affect the design of the website must be reflected in the design documentation. A reference list should be noted, as shown in Table 10.1 (a couple of example items are given based on our case study), and the relevant original BWD design documentation item(s) should be updated (and stored as new version(s)) for reference.

Table 10.1: Post-implementation amendments/enhancements

Change Description	Date	Original Documentation Item	Comments
Email link (on otherp.htm) needs updating to new email address	'Live'+4 weeks	Screen layout + webpage dialogue sheet	Existing email usable but new address would mean swifter checking
Quiz (isquiz.htm) needs refreshing for 'frequent' audience	'Live'+6 weeks	Screen layout + webpage dialogue sheet	Place additional quiz (not replace)
Post-implementation Amendments/Enhancements			
Website ID:	World Religions		
Date:	Week 12		

Chapter Exercises

Seminar Topics

1. Discuss the extent to which good marketing and promotion can make up for a poor website and the extent to which it matters which hosting option is chosen.
2. "My website audience will not want things to change all the time – they want it just the way they like the website." Discuss this statement, in particular if this approach is more relevant for certain website types, and the extent to which there is validity in taking this stance.
3. Build a set of points that justify having no online communications from or with your website users. Then identify the main possible drawbacks of this approach, especially for certain website types.

Tutorial Exercises

1. What main options are available for website hosting?
2. List the criteria that can be used to make an effective selection when choosing between hosting possibilities.
3. What are the main examples of website changes that could be needed following implementation?

Case Study

1. Make a list of key characteristics that you need in terms of your website hosting.
2. Match those needs to the hosting options available to you, choose the most appropriate provider, and choose the detailed attributes of the hosting offered.
3. Make a list of all possible ways that users can or might communicate with the website and/or people associated with the website, and detail a plan to make sure those communications are monitored and answered.
4. Write out a general plan for the promotion and long - term management of your website – including repair and growth.

INDEX

234

Index